Sandra,
May y
surrounded by the
white light of
protection and remain
true to your purpose.
Love,
Fatima Heath

One in Spirit

One in Spirit

By
Fatima Heath

E-BookTime, LLC
Montgomery, Alabama

One in Spirit

Copyright © 2009 by Fatima Heath

All rights reserved. No part of this book may be reproduced or transmitted in any form or by any means, electronic or mechanical, including photocopying, recording, or by any information storage and retrieval system, without permission in writing from the copyright owner.

Library of Congress Control Number: 2009901037

ISBN: 978-1-59824-993-4

First Edition
Published August 2011
E-BookTime, LLC
6598 Pumpkin Road
Montgomery, AL 36108
www.e-booktime.com

Do not believe in what you have heard;
do not believe in traditions
because they have been handed
down for many generations;
do not believe anything because it is
rumored and spoken of by many;
do not believe merely because the
written statements of some old sage are produced;
do not believe in that as truth to which you
have become attached by habit;
do not believe merely in the
authority of your teachers and elders.
After observation and analysis, when it agrees with
reason and is conducive to the good
and benefit of one and all, then
accept it and live up to it.

-Gautama Budda-

Contents

Acknowledgement 9

Introduction 13

Chapter One	*About the Author* 17
Chapter Two	*My Spiritual Journey* 24
Chapter Three	*The Little Church* 35
Chapter Four	*History of Spiritualism* 44
Chapter Five	*Jason, the Medium* 48
Chapter Six	*Contact With the Spirit World* 65
Chapter Seven	*Spirits from the Other Side* 79
Chapter Eight	*Philosophically Speaking* 87
Chapter Nine	*Class Development* 97
Chapter Ten	*Just a Thought Away* 107
Chapter Eleven	*Coincidence or Meant to Be?* 117
Chapter Twelve	*The Family is Everything* 127
Chapter Thirteen	*Our Church Family* 136
Chapter Fourteen	*The Purpose of it All* 143
Chapter Fifteen	*Some of My Favorite Mediums and Suggested Reading* 146

Hiding Man's Divinity 149

Acknowledgement

Thoughts are alive and your thoughts only die when you stop thinking them. Your loved ones die a physical death but live on in a spiritual world. They are only truly dead to you when you stop thinking about them, closing the door to their memory. They have things to accomplish in this spirit world and if you refuse to acknowledge their spiritual existence then they move on. When you think of them often, and keep their memory alive in thoughts and prayers they will remain close to you. They will help you in whatever way they can. Help from my family, friends and guides from the spirit side of life are very important to me. I never want to go without it. The choice is ours. We have control of spirit's presence in our lives.

Writing this book has been a dream of mine for several years. My hope is that the experiences and knowledge that you are about to read will awaken in you the truth about yourself. The truth is we do not die and that we continue to live in a spirit world. This book should remind you that you are made up of a human body, a mind, and most importantly a spirit. This book focuses on your spirit because that is the real you; an eternal you.

My wish in writing this book is that those of you who have had spiritual experiences, perhaps, similar to those in this book, may come forward without fear of being ridiculed. I would also like to see everyone use their spiritual gifts to their advantage. I do not feel that we use our intuition enough and that some of us do not acknowledge that we are intuitive. I also believe that we have healing gifts that can make people feel better. I firmly believe in the healing power of prayer, a hug, a smile, a kind word, or deed. In my opinion we are all psychic. Some of us choose not to develop this gift. Mediumship is another gift that we have the potential to develop if we so choose. Spiritualists call these gifts divine attributes.

This book could not have been written without the help of my many teachers and guides, both here on the earth plane and from the spirit side of life. I would like to thank all of those beloved souls on the earth plane who have trusted me with their personal experiences. I very much appreciate the spirit loved ones who have worked so diligently to prove the continuity of life after so called death. These spirits are friends, family members, teachers, and guides. I especially thank my nephew, Robert, who was a very old soul in a young man's body. He was a messenger on the earth plane and still is a messenger on the spirit side. It was Bobby's demise that left me searching for answers and comfort that he was at peace. I found truth and a life eternal in the spirit land. I also give my love and gratitude to my development teachers of the past and present. I acknowledge all of my spiritual friends and students who sat with me in meditation circles and who have shared their love, light, energy and knowledge so that I may progress on my spiritual quest. Sometimes, I was the student and they were the teacher. My deepest love and appreciation go out to my husband, Brian, and my children, Justin and Kimberlie, who have encouraged me and believed in me always. I would also like to acknowledge, my son Justin, for helping me edit and write this book. Much thanks to Jason McCuish who contributed one of the best chapters to the book. Last, but by no means, least, I must acknowledge the "Infinite Intelligence" which most call God. Without the knowledge that this all powerful and all knowing Intelligence exists, life would have little meaning.

Introduction

I am a Reverend and was the pastor of the Swampscott Church of Spiritualism in Swampscott, Massachusetts for several years. Spiritualism is a science, philosophy and religion of continuous life, based upon the demonstrated fact of communication by means of mediumship, with those who live in the Spirit World. A Spiritualist is one who believes in the communication between this world and the world of spirit by means of mediumship and who tries to mould his or her character and conduct by the highest teachings derived from such communication. The last twenty years of my life have been spent reading hundreds of books on metaphysics from many authors such as Ruth Montgomery, Edgar Cayce, Arthur Ford, Andrew Jackson Davis, Emanuel Swedenborg and more.

Concern for my sister who was grieving the loss of her young son started me on a spiritual quest in search of answers about life after death. This search took me to bookstores, psychics, meditation classes with gifted mediums, and most importantly, the religion of Spiritualism. It was here I met a Lynn, Massachusetts medium, who I believe to be one of the best mediums of our time. I have been in the company of many well known mediums from the United States and Great Britain and I believe that there are few that can compare to Jason in spirituality and natural ability of his mediumship. Jason gives very detailed messages that leave no one in doubt as to who the spirit is that is coming through.

This book is about my spiritual journey as well as many persons' spiritual experiences. I found much more than I was looking for. I found what I believe to be the answer to the God connection and the real you, which is so much more than you know. If we are only thinking with our earth-mind consciousness, we are missing out on the purpose of the earth plane life and how it connects to the God spark which is in all of us. The main reason for this book is to awaken us to the Spirit World, and to help you realize that we are first and always spirit.

One in Spirit is inspired by books that I have read, religious services that I have attended, material given to me in the dream state, shared experiences and readings from friends, mediums, meditation and philosophy classes. All of the experiences and messages in this book are factual. The names of the persons are sometimes changed in order to keep their privacy.

Often, I would ponder a question and shortly after would receive guidance that answered that question. Sometimes, it was answered in a book, the newspaper, a magazine, or on the television. Other times answers might come during a lecture, church service, or in a meditation circle. What is important is that the question always got answered to my satisfaction and to my surprise. This taught me a lesson which was "search and you shall find" or "ask and you shall receive."

Not everyone will want to be awakened to the real you; your spirit. Once you choose to be awakened to Spirit you will have no choice but to take on the responsibility of your own happiness or unhappiness according to spiritual and physical universal laws. This is a great responsibility to take on; however, it is necessary to your spiritual growth and to your journey into perfection with the God spark that we are all working to achieve.

When you read this book; many of you will identify with these stories on a personal level but would never speak of them for fear that you would be ridiculed. One father feels the presence of his deceased son. He watched an ethereal form come down the stairs after leaving his son's room. Another family hears an angelic choir stepping into a Creedence Clearwater Revival tape that was playing at the time two young men were killed in an automobile accident.

I am hoping that this book will help you realize that you are "One in Spirit". My hope is that all your fears of death will be eliminated and that you will look within for answers to your questions. Develop your own ability to communicate with your loved ones and guides on the spirit side of life. The wonderful philosophy of Spiritualism and spiritual experience has inspired me and it can also inspire you to look for the truth that we all live on. Most importantly, this book is about becoming more spiritual in your every day life by remembering that you are spirit and always will be spirit. Your true home is in the Spirit World and you will return to that world. Death should be viewed as a natural part of life, as a new beginning, and continued opportunity for growth and reform. This book consists of spiritual experiences and messages from loved ones that have passed on to the spirit side of life, spiritual philosophy, instructional guidance to your spiritual journey and more. The message is clear that we do not die but that we live and grow in a spirit world filled with love, hope, and eternal life. This book is about the real you; which is "One in Spirit".

Chapter One

About the Author

As a child, I have always sensed a presence around me. This left me with a feeling of peace and protection. There were many times when I felt guided to do something but I did not know why. I know, now, that I was always intuitive and I have a keen sense of right from wrong. I have always loved my private time and I have always felt comfortable with who I was and where I was going. I never gave much thought to my future but rather trusted that things would work out fine. My religious background was that of Roman Catholicism. My husband Brian was a Congregationalist Protestant who converted to Catholicism before we were married in 1970. Brian believed that being a good person was more important than what religion you belonged to. What was important to Brian was that we were all the same religion. My two children, Justin and Kimberlie were born and raised as Catholics. Catholics believe in saints, angels, and life after death; therefore, the idea of life after our physical death was very acceptable to me. The feeling of spirit presence, to me, was more about my guardian angel looking after me rather than a deceased grandmother or loved one that might be around me.

I never doubted that there was a God, but had always questioned the definition of God. I knew that God was good and that God was not responsible for bad things that happened to people. I never believed in a hell or that God punished people. The God that I believed in was a God that wanted the best for all of his children with no exceptions. God was unconditional love. I intuitively felt that a father would not love one child more or less than another child.

As a child, I tried to imagine what heaven was like. All I got for answers were that there were angels that would play beautiful instruments and that they floated on fluffy, white clouds. I was told that there was a judgment day, and only the worthy Catholics would sit with God in heaven. I remember thinking that sitting on clouds all day would be boring and I just wanted to be with my friends. Much of what Catholics believe in is based on faith. Roman Catholicism teaches that there is one eternal God, who exists as the trinity of three persons: the Father; the son, Jesus and the Holy Spirit. Catholics have faith that the Eucharist or communion is changed into the body of Christ. Catholics have faith that they were born with original sin. They also believe that all people have an opportunity for forgiveness and freedom from sin through Baptism. Catholics also have faith that Jesus had risen from the dead. Catholics have faith in Jesus Christ and his teachings and their mission is to spread the faith across the world.

Growing up as a teenager, I often thought about Catholicism and how Catholics viewed God. Catholicism put an emphasis on the fatherhood of God. Jesus Christ was the savior and the son of God. If you acknowledged Jesus Christ as the savior and you abided by the rules of the Catholic Church, then you would have salvation. The Catholic Church left no room for salvation in other religions. I was taught in Catholicism that if you were not a Catholic, you would not enter the kingdom of heaven. This teaching became quite an issue when a family member married outside of the Catholic Church. You were forbidden to attend a wedding of a Catholic and a non-Catholic. This marriage was not recognized in the eyes of the Catholic Church. I could not understand this way of thinking. It just never felt right to me. I always felt that it was better to be a good person that was not a Catholic rather than a bad person who happened to be a Catholic. Catholics go to confession in order to confess their so called sins. This is the process in which they are forgiven. You would go to church, preferably, once a week and go into a private box in order to tell the priest your sins. The priest would give you forgiveness and ask you to pray. You would repeat this process as often as you needed it. You could even kill someone and be forgiven by God. Reflecting back to my childhood and teenage years, that way of thinking did not really make sense. It certainly does not make sense, now, after all I have researched and experienced. I feel the necessity to express the way I was thinking as a child and what I was being taught, at that time. My way of thinking changed as I got older and wiser and more experienced with life and people.

I grew up in the 1950s and 1960s and divorces were not common amongst Catholics. My dad, Antonio was divorced from his ex-wife who lived in Portugal. He then married my mother, Hilda. The church never recognized this marriage even though my parents had five children that were all raised as Catholics. The nuns told us that our parents were sinners. Looking at it from the eyes of a child, this was very hard to understand. My parents were both from very devout Catholic families; nevertheless, they were liberal in their belief system and the thought of going to hell did not seem to bother them.

My father, Antonio, was quite an influence on my belief system because he was more liberal than my mother in what he believed about Catholicism. My father was comfortable with his belief system and he often told my sisters, brother and me stories of angels and the afterlife. My father was born in a little town in Portugal called Ilhavo and he was one of thirteen children. His father and mother were poor but proud people. His mother, Rosa Jesus, was very devoted to Catholicism. My father always spoke of my grandmother being the first one to open the church doors in the morning and the last one to close the doors in the evening.

The story that my father told about his teenage sister dying of an illness was the story that influenced me most as a child. My father recalled his mother grieving and praying so much for this child after she died that the child appeared to her mother. She begged her mother to stop grieving so that she could get on with her life in the spirit side of life. She wanted her mother to be happy and to stop crying for her because she was alive in the spirit world and needed to be freed from her mother's sadness and grief. My grandmother, Rosa, stopped her grieving. My father would remind us often of the story of the three children at the shrine of Fatima in Portugal. The Blessed Mother Mary appeared to these children and gave them messages to give to the World. These stories and others impressed me and made me very curious about this spirit world.

    Looking back on my childhood, my first experience with a psychic person took place when I was around ten years old. I sat at the kitchen table listening as Marjorie, a friend of the family, read tea leaves for the adults. My sisters and I were fascinated by these readings, which in time would prove to be true. We could hardly wait until we were old enough to have our tea leaves read and get messages about our future. Marjorie was a tenant who lived on the first floor of my parents five unit home. I spent much time with this woman. She taught me the joy of sitting outside on the stoop and gazing at the stars. She taught me to swim, and she taught me that there was more to the physical reality we knew because of her gift of prophecy. Marjorie taught me that we had a sixth sense known as our psychic ability. I thought this woman was so smart and that she knew everything there was to know. Marjorie was a great influence on me and I realize that she was in my life for a reason. This was the beginning of my introduction into a different reality from Catholicism. She was a Protestant.

My life really changed when I met my husband, Brian, a Congregationalist Protestant. I was just sixteen years of age. We met at a gathering at a friend's house. It was love at first sight for both of us and we both knew, intuitively, that we would someday marry. We only dated a few times and I did not hear from Brian until two years later. During this time, I could not stop thinking of him. I would cut out articles in the newspaper about him as captain and quarterback of his High School football team. I can recall my sister, Lucinda, saying "What are you doing that for?" "You will never see him again." My response was that I would someday marry him. Brian phoned me for a date a year after we stopped dating and my pride got in the way. I waited another year before I accepted. Brian told me that he was scared because he felt such a strong connection to me and he was only sixteen. He said that he could not stop thinking of me and it made it difficult for him to date. I felt the same way. We were married at twenty years old. My intuition was correct.

Brian never wanted religion to be an issue so he converted to Catholicism for me. He was baptized, and confirmed a Catholic. It was important that our future family would belong to one religion; otherwise, the Catholic Church insisted that Brian would agree to sign our children over to the Catholic Church to be raised as Catholics. Brian was at peace with this decision and it was very comforting to me. A year later, our son, Justin, was born and two years later, our daughter, Kimberlie was born.

The next fourteen years or more were very busy years as Brian and I spent time involved in sports with our children, running a real estate office, opening a restaurant with my in-laws, opening two hair salon businesses with a friend and my getting an associates degree in Business Management. I was on overload but I was happy doing what I felt was necessary for our future. I learned to follow my gut feeling even though there were times that my family thought I was crazy. My family was concerned that I was doing too much. My husband and I both thought that we had our priorities straight and we felt that we were doing the right thing by working hard and getting ahead, financially. I almost felt that things were out of my control and that opportunities were being placed in front of us for a reason. Brian had learned to trust my instincts. I had become a successful real estate broker and a good business woman. We were successful in the restaurant and hair salon businesses. Brian and I both had a lot of energy. My two children were now in their teens. As a family, we worked hard and we played hard. College was fast approaching and we were getting ready. There was little time for thoughts of a philosophical nature.

Chapter Two

My Spiritual Journey

The year was 1985 and I could feel my thoughts and interests starting to change. Winter had arrived and I was tired from a busy year in Real Estate. It was a particularly cold winter and I kept warm sitting by the wood burning stove reading one book after another. Television never interested me. My preference was reading. For some reason, not known to me, I felt an obsession with my reading. It was very comfortable and cozy to sit by the fire and read in my spare time. Books on metaphysics, ghosts, unidentified flying objects, books on various religions including Buddhism, Confucianism, Hinduism, the Egyptian worship etc. appealed to me. I was given a book on Spiritualism and the Fox sisters, but was not ready to grasp the concept, at that time. Most of the time I enjoyed reading all Ruth Montgomery's books, Edgar Cayce's material and Arthur Ford's books. These books were about famous psychics, healers, and mediums.

    I found myself fascinated with people who were gifted in prophecy and healing. I liked reading books on life after life. My religious belief system was changing, and these books were helping me to answer questions that I had about my own intuition. The mysticism in the Bible always intrigued me. My interests in the metaphysical field lead me searching for psychics, mediums, past life regression, and hypnotists etc. I found that some of these persons were very good and some were just hit or miss. I was aware that there were many frauds in the psychic field. I never had high expectations if I was going to see a medium for the first time. It was always a joy when I did get a good reading from a gifted psychic or medium. I also believed that we had "free will" and that we had the ability to change many things for the better or for the worse, depending on our actions and what we choose. Free will comes from my Catholic belief system. Spiritualism also teaches us that we chose our destiny and that we create our own happiness or unhappiness by our actions.

It was July 15, 1986 when my sister, Lucinda, phoned me to tell me that our nephew Robert was dead from a drug overdose. My life, the way I knew it, was about to change. I was not prepared for the spiritual journey that I was about to embark on. We called my nephew Bobby. He was just twenty-one years old and in the prime of his life. Bobby had a good job, an apartment, a motorcycle, truck, and life seemed filled with excitement and promise. Our city was experiencing an epidemic of drug overdoses at this time. The entire family was in shock because there were absolutely no signs of Bobby's involvement with drugs. Bobby was new in experimenting with drugs and his body was too virgin to handle the chemicals that were foreign to his body. My sister, Anna, and her husband Robert were devastated by the loss of their son. They both felt guilty because they had been blind to and missed any signs of Bobby's drug use. There was no way to ease their pain. My sister started to waste away before our eyes. Anna went to a local priest for answers and comfort but there were no words that would console her or ease her pain.

My sister, Anna, was losing a lot of weight and becoming very depressed. These things along with her insomnia, dilated pupils, rapid heart rate, and an inability to hold down food were symptoms of a thyroid condition. I was just twenty-one years old when I had developed a thyroid condition myself. I had a stressful job that I did not like and believe this stressful situation had triggered my own condition. I asked my sister if her doctor had tested her for a thyroid condition. She did not know. I urged her to ask her doctor to have the test done if she had not had one. I knew my sister thought I was a little crazy for insisting on her having this test. Anna did ask her doctor to test for thyroid when she found out she had not been tested for an over active thyroid. The doctor was very surprised when the results came back positive. The thyroid condition was so serious that my sister needed to take a nuclear pill and was quarantined for over twenty-four hours. The doctor was very apologetic and said she thought my sister's symptoms were due to the grieving of her son's death. She never thought to test for a thyroid condition. The doctor was curious and she asked Anna if I was a nurse. My sister said, "No she is a real estate broker." Learn to trust your intuition. Don't be worried about being wrong or what people might think. If the results came back negative I would have felt like nothing ventured nothing gained, but they came back positive and my sister was healed.

My obsession with reading books just a year prior to Bobby's death had come in handy. There was one book, in particular, that Anna felt a connection with. The book was "The Other Side" by James A. Pike, a well-known Bishop who communicated with his son after his son committed suicide. Mr. Pike's son was able to communicate through poltergeist occurrences and also through mediums. Anna, Robert, and the family were beginning the process of healing. Anna would read a book and call me to discuss it. I felt that my sister's sadness was diminishing as she gathered strength from these books and the hope that there was a life after death. Anna was on the road to recovery and she was able to move on with her life. Support from her other children and family made life bearable as she tried to make sense out of something so senseless.

Anna was becoming educated to the spirit side of life from the many books that she was reading. I believe it was because she and her family were open to the spirit world, that they made them able to experience the physical phenomenon that was happening around their home. One day, my brother-in-law, Robert, looked out into the hallway from his bedroom to see an ethereal shadow coming out of Bobby's room and continuing down the stairs into the living room. Bobby's presence was very strong in the house. The family dog, Tabatha, reacted to that presence. Tabatha never got along with

Bobby when he was alive. Bobby preferred larger dogs, particularly, ones he could take hunting. When Bobby was alive and entered a room Tabatha was in she would leave with her tail between her legs, shaking all the way. After Bobby's death, this same scenario continued to happen. The family would hear footsteps, and feel a presence but no one was there, physically. Several of Bobby's friends were having vivid dreams about Bobby. In the dreams, he warned his friends about taking drugs and the dreams continued for a long while. My family's interest was piqued and we started to search for someone who could communicate with the deceased.

My family and I were familiar with the term psychics and what they did. We had never heard of the term medium. We did not know what the difference was between the two. I now know that a psychic is a person who attunes to the vibrations of the universe. A medium is a person who is sensitive to the spirit vibration and through the medium intelligences in the spirit world is able to communicate messages. We were looking for a medium but we did not know this, then.

My sister, Anna, decided to see a psychic-medium that was recommended to her by a friend. Her name was Barbara. She brought Bobby through, immediately. Barbara became very emotional as she spoke of his passing and the addiction to drugs. She spoke of persons who were involved with him before his passing and Barbara spoke of experiences that were happening in the house. Some of these experiences were not even known to my sister.

Barbara confirmed that Bobby was very close to his brother, Michael, and that he was able to communicate with Michael by playing around with the radio. Michael and Bobby had shared the same room growing up, but listened to different radio stations. After Bobby passed to spirit, Michael would go to bed with his favorite radio station but would wake up to Bobby's favorite station on his radio. Michael was in denial that this could happen. He never mentioned it to his mother. Michael was very surprised when his mother confronted him about it. Michael said, "How do you know about this? I never told anyone." Michael was about thirteen when his brother passed away and this experience affected him profoundly. Michael was a quiet boy and kept everything inside him. How his mother could have known about the radio was a puzzle to him. Barbara had given my sister information about the drugs that were in Bobby's body before the test results had been revealed. Later, the information was confirmed.

The meeting was very comforting to my sister. Barbara advised Anna to go to the First Spiritualist Church of Salem, where she was a member. Barbara felt that Anna could receive more answers to her many questions there. At last, my sister, Anna felt that there was hope that Bobby's spirit was alive and well and living on the other side and that his life, which was short lived, had not been in vain.

My sisters, Anna and Lucinda, my mother, and I were about to embark on a journey of knowledge about the spirit world. We had decided to visit the First Spiritualist Church of Salem in Salem, Massachusetts.

Salem is famous for stories of witches. Innocent Christians were persecuted and hanged for so-called crimes of witchcraft in 1692. This helped to create an even more mysterious backdrop to an already intriguing introduction into the Spiritualist religion.

My family and I arrived early Sunday evening around 7:00 P.M. not really knowing what to expect. We sat down in a pew in a little church that looked much like any other church. There was a picture of Jesus, looking up to the heavens, hanging on the wall. A Bible and Spiritualist manual were on the lectern and in all I felt really good.

To start the service we sang a song from the hymnals that were placed in the front of the pews. The chairperson announced the speaker for the evening, whose name was Ellen, and then gave the invocation. In the front cover of the hymnals was the Declaration of Principles, which we read out loud. These Principles were taken from the Spiritualist manual:

1. We believe in Infinite Intelligence.
2. We believe that the phenomena of nature, both physical and spiritual are the expression of Infinite Intelligence.
3. We affirm that a correct understanding of such expression and living in accordance therewith constitute true religion.
4. We affirm that the existence and personal identity of the individual continue after the change called death.

5. We affirm that communication with so-called dead is a fact, scientifically proven by the phenomena of Spiritualism.
6. We believe that the highest morality is contained in the Golden Rule: "Whatsoever ye would that others should do unto you, do ye also unto them".
7. We affirm the moral responsibility of the individual and that he makes his own happiness or unhappiness as he obeys or disobeys Nature's physical and spiritual laws.
8. We affirm that the doorway to reformation is never closed against any human Soul here or hereafter.
9. We affirm that the precepts of prophecy and healing are divine attributes proven through mediumship.

After this they read of church events and we stood to sing another song from the hymnals. Then the speaker gave a wonderful talk, which was inspired by spirit. She spoke from the heart and had no notes to read from. The talk was about creating our own happiness or unhappiness by the choices that we make. I remember enjoying her talk very much. Next, the chairperson, Phyllis, announced that there would be a collection taken up for the church. Phyllis emphasized that you should only give a donation if you could afford to. I was so impressed by this and the fact that there was no lecture about the financial needs of the church. As a member of the Roman Catholic Church I often felt there was too much emphasis on what the church expected of its' collections. It was different here. The members were more concerned with making everyone feel comfortable and welcomed that what religious background you have or how much you can put in the collection plate. What happened next was very different than any mass I had ever attended. After an offering prayer, Ellen began giving messages to people in the pews. Ellen had my full attention. I observed that before she came to a person she would ask, "May I come to you?" Everyone was receptive and pleased as they seemed to respond positively to the messages being given. Ellen asked if she could come to me. I was surprised and pleased at the same time. Ellen said, "I have a little dog that is white with black spots and wiry fur. This dog was quite stubborn. The dog is saying that it had a good life and that he passed to the spirit side of life just a few years ago. The dog is telling me to tell you not to worry about him. This dog's energy is part of something special happening around your home." I knew that dog and the excitement of which she spoke. Ellen explained that animals live on also. They often step in to give you protection and comfort. Ellen left me with the blessings of Spirit and she went on to give a message to another person.

    By now, my family was all smiles. They remembered I had purchased a wire-haired Fox Terrier named Nino. This dog was stubborn, and he would not obey. The neighborhood cats were petrified of this dog. Nino often got loose and would jump right through screen doors to get at a cat. My husband and I gave the dog away. A woman who was passing by my house stopped to admire the dog. She told me that she had a twelve year old son who would love a dog like Nino but that they could never afford that type of dog. I said, "The dog is yours." My children were very young and they had no attachment to the dog at all. It was easy for us to give him up. I packed a bag with Nino's toys, brush, pills and treats and off the dog went with its new owner to live in New York. I often wondered if the dog had a good life and what had become of him. The excitement around my house had to be that our new dog, Molly, might give birth to puppies any minute. Molly was a beautiful, gentle, dachsund. The whole family was ready for this dog when we purchased her. The children were much older and loved her very much. This was so incredible. Ellen gave several more messages to other people in the church and then the service ended with a prayer. After the service, I had the opportunity to thank Ellen for the lovely message and lecture. I told her that the details in the message were accurate and that I understood about the excitement at home.

In the car on the way home, my mother, my sisters and I talked about what we had just experienced. I knew that most people would find this unbelievable, but seeing is believing. None of us knew any of those Spiritualists and none of them knew us or that we would be attending this service. How did Ellen know about my dog, Nino, and the guilt that I felt when I gave him up? We had gone to the church expecting to hear from my nephew, Bobby, but heard from my old dog instead. This made us laugh quite a bit during the car ride home and laughter can be very healing for the soul. My family felt it had been an interesting experience, but weren't touched in the same way that I was.

Later, from the back of a pamphlet I had gotten from the church, I read and thought about each Declaration of Principles of Spiritualism. I found it profoundly comforting.

Chapter Three

The Little Church

I could not wait to get back to the Little Church in Salem. I picked up a few books on the Fox sisters and read how they were responsible for the era of Modern Day Spiritualism. I felt a need to know more about this religion of Spiritualism before my second visit. I tried to convince my sisters and mother to go with me. They were not interested in going again even though they found it fascinating. I remained excited about returning to the First Spiritualist Church of Salem even though it meant going there alone. I arrived a few minutes early and looked around observing everyone. The service was enjoyable, but I did not get a message this time. I had learned from the church announcements that there was an early service at 5:30 P.M. and that it was an all message service. This service was primarily for the members of the church that were developing their ability as mediums. I thought this would be worth coming to. In addition to the early service there was a half hour of sociability, which took place downstairs from the church. After the sociability, there was a short healing service, and then the main church service started at 6:45 P.M. I knew that the following week, my third visit, I would go early at 5:30 P.M. and stay till the end. I was already looking forward to my next visit.

    The following week I arrived early, again. I was anxious for the opportunity to speak with anyone who would listen to me and, perhaps, enlighten me as to what this religion was all about. After the early service, I went downstairs into the church basement for a light dinner. There was a variety of sandwiches, sweets, and beverages for a small donation. I helped myself to a sandwich and coffee and sat down next to a gentleman who appeared to be my age. I introduced myself and told him that I was new to the church and did not really know what to expect. He told me that his name was Lenny and that he had been coming to the church for over a year.

    Lenny said that finding this church was a God sent for him. He was a natural psychic as a young child and he had many questions himself. Lenny was encouraged to develop his psychic ability as a child. His mother understood this gift, but she discouraged Lenny from speaking about it outside the house. Lenny found it difficult to keep this secret as a child. He also felt that there must be something wrong with this ability if he could not speak of it to anyone outside the house. He always felt different from the other children. Lenny told me that he knew things were going to happen before they happened. I had read about this and I knew that it was called precognition. Lenny was clairvoyant, clairsentient, and clairaudient. He explained that he was able to see, hear and sense spirit. Lenny had also experienced levitation. He confessed that having these gifts were not always fun. Controlling this gift was a problem. There were many times when Lenny had to keep things from his friends, loved ones and teachers and it made him feel that he was different from his peers. Lenny was a very sincere and likeable person and I took to him right away. Lenny was also raised as a Roman Catholic. We had this experience in common, and I was pleased that I had met someone with whom I could talk. Once again I looked forward to my return next week.

    I had plenty of food for thought during the next week, and often thought of the church and my new acquaintance, Lenny. I went back to the library for more books on psychics, and spirit communication. The more I read the more questions I had. I was learning many new words and the definitions of these words. I was embarking on the shores of a whole new world, that of the spirit world. I was able to find time to read at night before sleeping because my days were so filled with the many businesses that my husband and I were involved with. My work never suffered because of my new found interest. If anything, I felt that it helped me. I worked harder and faster to get things accomplished so that I had more time to read.

    My friend Lenny had become a member of the First Spiritualist Church of Salem and had joined a church development class. This is a class for persons who are interested in developing their psychic sense. He was taking the next step with his natural abilities and trying to become a true medium. It is not easy to develop as a medium. I am told that we are all mediumistic;

however, the time, effort, and practice that it takes to develop as a medium makes it impossible for many to reach the end result. Practice makes perfect is true when studying to be a medium. It is not unusual for development to take years. I looked forward to attending the early services because I had a better chance of getting a message. The early service was not heavily attended. I particularly hoped for a message from Lenny because I found him to be very evidential. The thought of being a medium was so incredible to me. For the first time in my life, I was thinking about life after death and communication with the so-called dead. I constantly questioned this belief and I always came away with some proof that this was for real. Many times throughout the week I would be heavy in thought about a situation in my life and that week in church the lecture would happen to be on that same subject. I can remember thinking of my grandmother Rosa all one week, and at church that Sunday she came to me with a kind word. Sometimes, I would receive a message from a spirit loved one and it was as though the medium was reading my mind. Week after week, I went to that little church and felt privileged to have been let in on such a wonderful secret.

My husband was most understanding of my new adventure into this world of spirit but he cautioned me often about discussing my experiences at the church with just anybody. Brian made it his job to make sure that I kept my feet on the ground and that my credibility was kept intact. I remember one time. I was discussing life insurance with a salesman and I mentioned that I believed in life after death. I told him that I had found this religion that believed in communication with the dead. The expression on the salesman's face change and I knew that he thought I was crazy. My husband told me later that I should find another way to phrase the fact that my church communicated with the dead. He thought most people would think of séances and Ouija boards etc. I have learned to say that Spiritualists believe in life after death and communication with those who have passed to the spirit side of life through thought telepathy, intuition, and the use of gifted mediums. Brian was more concerned about people's reaction than I was. He would give me a little kick under the table if he thought I should change the subject. Brian attended a few services. He was intrigued, understanding, supportive, and protective all at the same time.

Sometimes, I would get a message from a medium who would ask me to relay a message to someone that I knew. Once, a medium asked me to convey a message to Hilda from Antonio who was in the spirit side of life. The message was "My brother would be fine and that he was sending him healing." My mother's name is Hilda. My brother was ill and my mother prayed that he would recover. This message was from my Dad, Antonio, and proved to be very evidential. My brother did recover. I did not always feel that I could relay messages to everyone that I received messages for, because not everyone's belief system would allow a message to get through.

Hollywood movies sometimes portray Spiritualism in a spooky light. This is not what Spiritualism is about.

Today, Spiritualism is growing as people find the need to connect with their loved ones. There are good mediums and there are frauds.

The Spiritualist religion tries hard to educate and train persons for mediumship. There is a certificate one must receive in order to be accepted as a certified medium from a Spiritualist Church. This certification requires attending an acknowledged development class from certified teachers. It is mandatory to take lessons from a reputable learning Institute such as Morris Pratt Institute in Wisconsin and necessary to pass a written test and a mediumship demonstration which is accepted by a panel of certified mediums. I wouldn't be honest if I said that all the mediums that I have come in contact with were accurate. Most were truly doing the work of spirit, honestly and sincerely, but there have been a few mediums I've known who were both egotistical and general in their message work. There are many exceptional mediums that are evidential beyond a doubt.

Delivering an evidential message from the spirit side of life with unmistakable detail is what sets mediums apart. An example of an evidential message might be: "I have your uncle Jarred here and he tells me that he traveled with a circus when he was on the earth plane. He says that you have done your share of traveling and that you will still have a lot more to go before you are settled in your career." This kind of a message would be hard to discard as a hoax. The key being that, even though the person giving you the message knows nothing about you, they give you the evidence of truth with a fact or detail only someone who knew you well would know. A more general

One in Spirit

message might sound like this, "I have your grandmother here. She says, "She loved you and use to cook and bake a lot when you were young." "She would like to tell you she's proud of you." This message, although positive, does not give the recipient any real detail that can be proved beyond a reasonable doubt. That message could be from just about anyone's grandmother. Keep in mind that spirit wants their message to be received, and a good medium will always provide the evidence for the presence of that spirit.

I once received a message from a very gifted medium named Ida. She told me that my grandmother was there and that she had brought a rose that was symbolic. Well, my dad's mother was named Rosa Jesus and she was very close to me when I was a baby. My grandmother told me that in time I would be lecturing and giving messages from the pulpit. She also told me it would not come easy and that I would go kicking and screaming the entire way. I was also told never to doubt my gift because I was guided by many on both sides of life. This same medium, Ida, told me that I was involved in many professions and that I would continue to do many different things in my life until I felt I had found the right career for me. She explained that it was like trying on many pairs of shoes until you get the right fit. She said that once I got the perfect fit; I would know it. At the time, I didn't believe that message to be true even though the evidence of spirit was so strong. I hated public speaking and had no intentions of developing as a medium. I was, however, fascinated by psychics and the Spirit World. I laughed all the way home, but just five short years later I was a member of the First Spiritualist Church of Salem and a part of a medium development class.

Today, I am a pastor of the Swampscott Church of Spiritualism where I lecture and give messages. Ida was also right about the many professions that I would be involved in. I was a secretary, day care giver, home health aide, restaurant owner, hair salon partner, real estate investor and real estate broker. I have certainly tried on many pairs of shoes and I have, finally, found the right fit. I enjoy selling real estate and serving the members of the Swampscott Church of Spiritualism. I receive evidential messages from my nephew Bobby, my nephew Alec, my father, Antonio, my grandmother, Rosa, and my mother-in-law, Pauline, as well as many more spirits that come through to help guide me on my journey.

At the time of Ida's message, my life was changing in many different ways. The friends and people who I had surrounded myself with no longer held the same appeal. My interests were changing, and we had less and less in common. This is probably true of most people who experience a profound spiritual growth in a very different direction than their friends. I was beginning to appreciate the simple things I had taken for granted. I had always known the importance of getting a good job and earning enough to live a comfortable life, but now the accumulation of material things seemed a lot less important. I began caring about things of a more philosophical nature. My family's happiness and health became my biggest goal. My children were in college at the time and I didn't want them choosing careers just for the financial rewards. I wanted them doing things that made them feel good about themselves. It was also around this time that they began to take an interest in the church and attended a few services. I really cared about my children doing things in life that they would enjoy and that they would feel good about. I did not want them to take a job just for the money they would earn. I always stressed the importance of staying healthy and happy to my children. My children were in college when they started to take an interest in my religion and started to attend a few services.

Chapter Four

History of Spiritualism

Throughout the ages human beings have been aware of spirits. Nearly all of the various forms of psychic phenomena associated with Spiritualism are as old as man. The Greeks consulted oracles and the Romans practiced divination to obtain guidance from the gods. Even today, there are cultures that have witch doctors who invoke the powers of the spirit for healing.

The early Christian Church was founded on the basis of mediumship. Spiritualists consider Jesus of Nazareth to have been one of the most gifted psychics and medium that ever walked the earth. I believe, he was the most gifted of the mediums. We need only to look to the Bible for his many miracles of healing, his prophecy and his inspirational teachings. The Bible in both the Old and New Testaments has many references to psychic abilities.

The 4th century Council of Nicaea brought to an end the use of mediums and held that divine guidance through the Holy Spirit, was allowed only from the priesthood. It was around this time that the witch hunt became more popular. The persecution of people with psychic ability through the practice of these witch hunts received official religious sanction in 1484. During this long period of persecution anyone suspected of using psychic gifts was in danger of torture, trial and burning. Hundreds of thousands of mediums were put to death by organized "witch hunters". I can remember having bad dreams about people being burned at the stake and being dunked until they drowned. In these dreams I also remember families being persecuted. It was only a nightmare or was it a past life recollection? I will never know.

  The religion of Spiritualism was partly founded by writings of the Swedish mystic Emanuel Swedenborg in the 1700's. The unique feature of Spiritualism is the belief in life after life and communication with the so called dead by individuals with a gift for mediumship. Spiritualism developed in the 1840's to 1920's in the United States. By 1897 there were over eight million followers in the United States and Europe. The middle and upper classes were particularly drawn to this religion and many of the prominent Spiritualists were women. In the late 1880's the movement's credibility was hurt due to accounts of fraud being perpetrated by people calling themselves mediums. Because of this, religious organizations began to appear as a way to help protect honest mediums. Today, Spiritualism is primarily practiced through various denominations in Spiritualist Churches throughout the United States and United Kingdom.

  March 31, 1848 is known as the advent of Modern Day Spiritualism. On that day Kate and Margaret Fox of Hydesville, New York, reported that they had made contact with the spirit of a murdered peddler. This spirit communicated through rapping noises, audible to onlookers. This evidence appealed to practically minded Americans. The Fox sisters became an overnight sensation.

Most of the Spiritualists whom I know are free thinkers or free spirits. Spiritualists believe in allowing mankind to worship God in their own understanding and not in a particular or prescribed manner. We call God Infinite Spirit. The religion of Spiritualism encourages man to develop his spiritual gifts. Spiritualists also believe that we all have these gifts and that they are dormant within the individual. These gifts of prophecy, healing, and mediumship manifest themselves through visions, automatic writing, the laying on of hands, speaking in tongues, and trance, all giving us proof that there is a continuation of life after death. These gifts are universal, everlasting and have been witnessed over the ages in all parts of the world.

Spiritualism is a science and a philosophy, as well as religion. Spiritualists investigate and record the facts of spiritual manifestations. We discuss the existence of natural laws, fundamental beliefs and the reasons for them, as well as acknowledging the existence of an infinite intelligence as architect of our existence.

I have adhered to Spiritualism because of its common sense approach to religion in that it preaches personal responsibility. It has removed any fear I may have had of death. Spiritualism allows me to develop my own spiritual gifts while attuning to God. This religion makes me happy, gives me hope and upliftment. Spiritualism encourages me to reach my highest potential in everything that I do and to strive to be a better person. It is my belief that the world is in for a philosophical and spiritual shift that will help us answer the question of why we are here. It is also my belief that people are looking for an inner intuitive guidance for their lives that is truly spiritual.

Chapter Five

Jason, the Medium

The search for God is a curious adventure. Sadly, a lot of people go through life without ever looking; yet, God is staring them in the face. I found my God in a way that was very direct and different. There was no denying it because he was manifesting in my life, through the life of others with the help of loved ones who passed on. Today, I can say I am a medium. Then, I had no clue what that really meant. One of the most frequently asked question to a medium is probably, "When did it all start? How did you become a medium?" I would love to tell you that it had this fanciful and cool story attached to it, but that isn't really the story I tell. It is interesting nonetheless, but it is also unbelievable, challenging and every day it is more rewarding and uplifting.

    I am contributing this piece to Fatima's story not only because she asked me to, but also because I am a living and breathing testimony to the power of Spirit. Even more so, I feel that sharing a story about Spirit is a story worth telling. Many people overlook the power of mediumship in their lives. With a world full of trouble, turmoil and terror individuals all around the world are finally opening their eyes to the wonder and belief that life is continuous and we can find the proof of that while we are here – living! Sadly, many people will find ways to discredit, in their lives, the wonder that our loved ones are in fact living on, but it is real! It is wonderful! We are connected! They are connected! We are, in fact, one with God and our loved ones. We have all the tools within us that allow us to know that they are not gone and are around us everyday in every way. We just have to be open to that.

As I reflect on my life as a medium now for the past ten years, I realize that everything I have done has led to this path in my life. My work as a medium really came to its fruition when I was eighteen years old and in my second year in college. It wouldn't be fair if I tried to tell my story without telling you a bit of Jacob's story.

Jacob is my younger cousin. When he was about eight years old he was the living and breathing proof of M. Night Shyamalan's *Sixth Sense*. He walked right into the room where his parents were sitting to tell them that he was, in fact, seeing "dead people." Of course, you might think, he was influenced by the movie, but it didn't take long until this statement became more than true for all of us. We, as a family, decided to hold a séance to see if, in fact, there were any spirits in the home that he was seeing. With the experienced help of our family (my mother and her siblings who are all experts with dealing with the paranormal), we quickly realized that Jacob was, in fact, seeing something. I could go on, with a book in itself, telling you about the stories of Jacob, but there isn't enough time in one chapter. I did realize, then, that his experience was soon to become my experience too.

Prior to this experience I had many different encounters with what is deemed "paranormal" throughout my life, but sort of looked at them as the "creepy" ghost stories that I shared with my friends during "artificial" story time. They sure loved hearing them. I sure loved telling them. I remember being able to fill up hours with stories with many of my friends. They were not just stories of my experiences, but they were also stories of experiences my family had. Who would have known that Jacob's initiation of me into a séance would have created thousands of stories of their own about Spiritual experiences with me?

My life changed from that point forward. I began to see the world differently. I didn't experience anything at the séance but the feeling that there was so much more to the world. There was so much more to life than what we can see. I left Jacob's house that night in wonderment about what else there is to this thing we call life. I realized that there was so much more that needed explaining. Was I the one to find the answers? I sure didn't think that I would be finding all the solutions, but I wanted to investigate some of the problems, at that point, that Jacob was having. It didn't take long before I began to find answers.

It was about two weeks later that I found the answers in a way that I never imagined possible. One evening while sitting at home with my best friend, I had an experience that has been the driving force of my life ever since. As my best friend and I were sitting in my room watching a movie, I saw the presence of an individual sitting right next to me, in the chair to my right, at my computer. As I looked over I couldn't believe that what I was seeing was someone who surely didn't walk through the door. I, frantically, began to hit my friend and ask him if he was seeing what I was seeing. He was looking at me as if I was crazy. As if I had seen a ghost. Indeed, I was.

"Joseph, Joseph, please tell me that you are seeing what I am seeing?"

He looked at me in disillusionment. I instantly began to think of Jacob. I thought about the séance. I thought about all the stories that I had been telling for all those years. I began to think about all the stories that my mother shared with me. Is this what they have been talking about? Is this what I have been talking about? I was in awe.

As my head swiveled back and forth between Joseph and the Spirit I couldn't believe what was happening, then, the unthinkable. The Spirit began to speak. As I listened I told Joseph what he was saying. He was telling me and reliving all the experiences he had before he passed away. Joseph looked at me in disbelief. How was it possible that I was sharing any of this information with him and what was I talking about? Needless to say, after he disappeared Joseph validated all of the information to be his cousin who had passed away. I couldn't believe what happened. Was I going crazy? Was I imagining something unimaginable? It turns out I wasn't going crazy and I was imagining the imaginable. It was meant to be and so my spiritual path began to unfold and so did my life as a medium. Spirit found me. Jacob, Joseph and his cousin all lead me to the life that I now live; a life that has been fulfilled and has fulfilled the life of others with healing and closure for countless individuals who I have given readings to from their loved ones on the other side.

I thought it important you get the gist of who I am in order to understand the information I am going to share about mediumship. For the most part, what you have read above is a synopsis of my "Spiritual" life at this point. For a long time, I challenged and fought against myself working as a medium. It went against everything that religion had in store for me. To some extent, I really didn't have time to be a medium. My life was all worked out for me. I knew what I wanted and I was going for it. Amidst the turmoil of many deaths in my family I think that the beginning that Jacob created for me was the beginning of my life. The true beginning, the one that didn't exist from the womb, but the one in which my spiritual eyes, the one that God wanted me to see the world from, were finally open.

I realized with the experience with Joseph and his cousin that there was a lot of strength that can be derived from connecting with a loved one. It seemed to be true for Joseph. It began to be a new mission in my life. I wanted people to feel that connection with their loved ones. A connection that, realistically, I always wanted for myself with all of the loved ones who I lost. The day after the connection with Joseph's cousin there was no escaping my life as a medium. I realized that it gave him closure and love. It was as if magic created love. His closure with his cousin allowed his heart to heal. It was as if magic transformed him and me, both, at the same time.

I remember waking up the next day from speaking with Joseph's cousin wondering if he would ever talk to me again. I wondered if he would even look at me the same way anymore. At the time I gave Joseph my first reading, I worked in an after school age program for at risk youth as a full time job while attending college. It was upon my arrival at work that day that I realized this gift was not something to take for granted, but also something that needed some explanation.

That day was the first day of my new life. I say that, not in the sense that all that I had before was left behind, but it was as if a new life, one in which there were many new challenges imposed itself upon the life that I was already leading. It didn't change my path nonetheless, I still went to college, I still wanted to be a teacher, but there was so much more for me to do.

The beauty was that the new path allowed me at a young age to begin doing something that I always wanted to do – help people. It gave me purpose and fulfillment in a way that many young people, at my young age, could only hope to achieve; nonetheless, ever wanted to have in their life, at a time in a young college life, when the bars and hanging out to four in the morning drinking is the cool factor and important. Instead, I was allowed to transform individuals' lives in a way that I aspired to through teaching. It was through readings that people were allowed a moment, an instance, and a second or longer, to do one thing that they always wanted to do – have that one last connection and feel closure on the chapters of their book that they couldn't close. I had that ability. This is the path that I always wanted in my life, I wanted to help people. I wanted people, especially young people, to feel that their lives can move forward, always, even amidst the difficulty and curveballs that life always throws at us. Seeing Spirit allowed me to provide this closure; this support mechanism to all those who sought after me.

The truth is, for a long time I never had to seek anybody out to try my gift on. Spirits of those deceased, or passed on, were the ones who sought after me. They were always showing up in precarious situations with messages to those I would be around. For a long time, it didn't matter where I was. It could be the bar, at school, during a lecture with a professor, dealing with some of the younger students I was working with, no matter the situation Spirit manifested whenever and wherever they wanted. They were always present. I had no control over whether or not I wanted to receive their messages. They showed up, just like the family member who rings your doorbell and you don't want to answer because you just didn't want to talk to them, it didn't matter. They were, for a long time in my life, in control. There was no option as to whether to answer the door or not. They came barging right in. At work, at school, in the shower, or even while I was asleep. Even amidst the aggravation and frustration they caused, there was a light at the end of the tunnel. It wasn't necessarily for me; it was always for all of those that I shared the messages with. Their messages always seemed to be accurate. Their messages always seemed to be real. Just like the message to Joseph, all of the strangers at the supermarket, the bowling alley, on the street, or the friends who I creeped out, one thing was for sure, this so called "gift" was surely more than a blessing, but many times a burden.

I could tell you about all the times I predicted the lottery number (even against my fathers own belief), I could tell you about all the times I predicted the weather (to my mothers own joy and laughter) and I could tell you about the times I brought through, my now, sister-in-laws loved ones (even against my brothers own judgment), but all that is family. It is easy to discredit family and say, well, yeah, of course they will support you and agree with you, but it wasn't always that easy. I was always going against the grain with the work that I do. Whether it was friends or family, one thing was for certain, this gift caused a lot of my personal relationships with others to be strained and tried. It caused much confusion in my young life and made many people question the credibility I have, not only a medium, but also as an individual; however, the truth remains certain, all those who challenged, now understand. All those who were once in disbelief, now believe. All those who were just as confused as I once was, now find that the crowd of clouds that once fogged their judgment are now clear and the skies are all blue. No more of the storm of difference and discomfort that once existed. It is evident, that my ability, to touch in with the spirit world, is true and valid! I, truly, am capable of touching in with those who are gone or passed. Because truly they are never gone, with the help of a medium, but transfixed right upon us with their love, blessings and assistance nothing more than a thought away. My attempt in this little chapter is to provide you with this realization, through some of my profound and loving exposures with Spirit, which I wish to share.

One of the most difficult things when starting out on the path of seeing Spirit is making others believe. I, now, use the verb "make" because when I started out with this whole path in life that is all it was about. I wanted everyone to believe that I wasn't making this thing up. It's easier said than done. I found that fact out quickly. The fact of the matter is simple, no one really wants to believe you, it doesn't matter how much integrity or intelligence you have people want to doubt those things that they don't understand. Of course, it makes sense. I mean, hey, I was the same way. I doubted it too, how could I expect anyone else to believe what I was saying is true? Yet, I set out on a mission with Spirit to make those around me believe. This was the most important facet about Spirit communication. If others believed in me then I could believe in myself. I had it with Jacob. I had it with Joseph. I just needed it with everyone else that was around me. I just needed to find the language to introduce this new skill I had to others. I wanted to defray from the simple and Hollywood oriented statement that I could see dead people. I wanted to find a way in. How could I discuss it with others? How could I make them not look at me like I was not joking (not to mention I was a practical joker)?

One of my first readings came with a friend of mine named Rhiannon. Rhi (as her friends called her) was one of the employees with me at the after school program I worked at. When this whole world (the spiritual world) began to unfold before me, I realized that it was time this whole existence needed some proof, not only for me, but as I mentioned earlier, for those around me as well. Well, I got the proof.

As Rhi and I were hanging out one day, I noticed, a Spirit around her who wanted me to talk to her for him. I decided that I would take this chance, even if it meant risking our friendship. This was a common problem with me; I always felt that talking to Spirit was always risking the relationships I had already created with individuals. What if I was wrong? What if this "gift" wasn't anything more than me imagining things that weren't there? Well, I decided that I was pretty confident, and even according to my own better judgment, I would see if this individual was, in fact, someone who needed me to talk to her. So, I did.

Rhi and I were hanging out in the arts and crafts room when I first saw this young man around her. He was, just as we were, sitting patiently in the same room we were in. He was looking at her and watching her every move. I don't think he realized that I was important until he caught me staring at him.

It was at that moment that he looked at me and saw that I could see him. He, then, walked over to me and inquired whether I could see him. With about twenty kids in the room, I imagined that I couldn't see him, and made him imagine that I couldn't see him. It was interesting. I realized for the first moment, that they, like me, couldn't really tell that I could see them unless I validated to them that I could see them – Spirit. I ignored him for quite some time. Then later on, while we were just hitting the down time of the job, I decided that I would ask Rhi if I could talk to her in private and tell her about what I had seen. We found a private office in the building and I sat her down. I decided to investigate this belief in Spirit by asking her a series of questions: Have you ever had someone who had to tell you something that you didn't know how to tell them? Have you ever had to question the friendship you had with someone in order to make yourself feel better? I think, at this point, that she thought this was the beginning of me attempting to tell her I wanted to begin dating her; yet, this wasn't anything of the sort. When she responded yes, to all of my questions, I pursued. Well, I have to tell you that I am seeing "dead people" (the easiest way I knew how to tell people at that point), and I have someone around you who wants to speak with you. Do you mind if I tell you about him?

To my astonishment, Rhi was excited. She wanted to hear everything that I told her. I couldn't believe it. I didn't expect a happy response. She was all for it. She was the first person who really made me feel as if this "gift" was not a burden. She wanted to hear what I said. As I pursued this conversation I began to tell her about this individual whom I saw around her who was being circled, at his feet ironically, by a squirrel. It turned out, precisely, that his name was "squirrel" and that is what his friends called him, especially Rhi. The whole reading continued on. Rhi, honestly, by the end, was one of my biggest supporters and, of course, the strength that I needed to assist me in bringing my gift to all of those whom I have reached since I began this mission.

As I became more and more comfortable with my gift, I explored it more and more. There were friends I gave readings to. There were strangers I gave readings to. In fact, there were friends and strangers, many times, which I gave readings to at the same time. I have nearly never received a negative response. Truth be told, I am the biggest skeptic. I take every reading and every experience with "spirit" with a grain of salt. At least, that is what I did for a very long time. I was never really sure whether or not it was me or some fanciful illusion that was always right; however, as time ticked on and the readings multiplied, I realized there was definitely something to this gift. Since its conception, I have seen drug addicts turn reformed; I have seen people take solace and reconciliation with their loved ones; I have seen people find the strength to move on with their lives. Do I do all of this in order to scam or watch people believe in a nonexistent after-life? I think not.

Perhaps, the most evidential experience I had came about five years into my work as a medium. I attended a retreat by a well-renowned medium. I, at that point, had never met the man, nor did I know what was going to transpire. I sort of just went, because a dear adopted "Granny" (one of the most amazing people I could have imagined meeting on this spiritual journey) of mine brought me along with her. This experience transformed my belief in "spirit" and the things that we, together, were capable of.

The first night, at the retreat, this gentleman came over to me, with no prior knowledge of me or who I was, and said, "I know that you are capable of working as a medium and I would like you to take the stage with me on Thursday." Personally, I laughed to myself wondering how this man could assume to know anything about me; but, I guess that I was even more skeptical about him and the gift he presumed to have, than I did about my own; so, I figured I would humor him and agreed to go along with it. Honestly, when Thursday night rolled around, I was a nervous wreck. I didn't know what he was going to ask me to do, nor did I feel comfortable "taking the stage" with my gift in front of a crowd of people. I allowed my faith to take over. This was my only choice. One of the things that people believe in, all people, is that when you believe in God, he will not let you down. I did the same thing and assumed that whatever was supposed to happen was meant to be.

Thursday night rolled around. I was twitching in my skin. I couldn't believe that I agreed to put myself out there like I was about to, and for that matter, I still didn't know what was about to happen; yet, my Granny gave me confidence and love by telling me, "this is what you have been waiting for. You are going to show them the gift that you have been given and it is all meant to be." I honestly hated it, when people said things that were meant to be. I always felt in control over my own fate, yet, she was encouraging me, in a way, that said, *you really aren't in control. Just let what is meant to be, happen.* This was an eye-opening experience. It allowed me the realization that, whether we think we are in control, there is something bigger than all of us that wants us to reach our true potential. My "fate" was no longer influenced by my friends, my family, what others would say, how others would respond, what others might think, how my family would respond to this "psychic" putting the family name out there, what my friends would think of me, and how I thought of the stigma attached to myself doing this type of work; instead, I allowed myself to just "be" in that moment, without reservations, without constraint and constrictions, and said, "This is who I am now." With that in mind, I sat up on the stage in front of the crowd before me with no reservation and no knowledge of what was going to happen. I figured the worst case scenario would be that this man would ask me to talk to Spirit.

The man who asked me to be part of the demonstration began and I paraphrase, "Tonight we are going to try something different. I have before you a medium and I am going to challenge him in a way that he has never been challenged before." At this point not only were my palms sweaty, but I had nothing to lose, I thought about getting up and walking out; yet, my confidence and my belief in my ability took over. I stayed still, even, perhaps, against my better judgment. He continued (again I paraphrase), "in a few moments, I am going to ask Jason to leave the stage and enter another room, outside of this room. While he is in the other room, I am going to ask another medium, who I have pre-selected, to come up and give a reading to someone, anyone, in this room. Once that reading is said and done, I am going to ask Jason to come back into the room."

What the heck is going on? I was in wonderment. I was nervous. I was scared. Why was I going to leave the room? What was going to be expected of me? Not only were my palms sweaty but the nice suit I had worn was dripping with sweat. I could barely breathe as I walked out of the room. *Am I going to just try to give someone a reading?* I was already nervous enough about that, yet, my heart told me what I was about to do was so much more. I left the room. Part of me wanted to stand at the door and see what I could hear, but not only was someone outside of the room with me, but also my own faith took over and said, *whatever I am about to do is meant to prove something to me, not everyone else in that room.*

I remember staring out the window at the beach that sat before me. I took a deep breath. I laughed to myself and thought, if only my friends could see me now. I was twenty-six and about to talk to "spirit" in front of a large crowd. It was not what I expected. It was not what they expected. They, for the most part, were hoping to hear stories about my "Euro-trip" and I, as a young man, was hoping to fulfill their expectations with stories of excitement and enticement, but once again, the story they were expecting wasn't the story that I was about to tell; instead, my story was more about the experience I was about to have when I re-entered that room in front of a crowd of expecting participants.

I entered back into the room on cue. The moderator continued. "Jason, while you were out of this room, one of the participants in this crowd gave someone in here a reading. One of the participants was accurate and told someone in this crowd a message from someone they love and whom they have lost. Our expectation is, that you will be able to give that same person a message, tell them the same thing one of our mediums told them from the same person in spirit and, in the end, tell us who, in this crowd, gave that person a message." I gasped in disbelief. *Are they serious? Do they really think that I am capable of this?* I thought about making a break for it. There was no one here, besides my Granny, Sondra, who really knew me. What did I have to lose by leaving? What is this suppose to show? Did I have anything to prove? I realized, then, that this was an opportunity to prove something to myself, not anyone else. I sat there, I concentrated, and I felt that "spirit" showed up and wanted to work with me. I smiled.

I felt, at this point, everyone in the room was expecting me to fail. Although they probably weren't I couldn't help but feel that way. Maybe it was me who really expected to fail; however, I digress. Just as I sat there in serious disbelief, Spirit arrived and I stood up.

I scanned the crowd. As I was looking around I swore I heard a woman in the crowd yell, "It's me!" I thought to myself, well, there goes that experiment. She just ruined it by yelling out. Then I realized she didn't actually say anything. I was just in tune with my psychic senses and I laughed. It has to be her. I asked the lady permission to give her a reading and she willingly agreed. I might mention that not only had I never seen her before, but I haven't seen her since that day. I proceeded to read her. The reading went on for about ten minutes. Honestly, she was able to validate and recognize everything that I mentioned. I was in awe. It turned out that I gave her pretty much an identical reading that the other medium, who went on before me, had given. Everyone was aghast. Truth be told, did anyone actually think that I could give the same reading someone else already gave? It was impossible. I, through the work of Spirit, made things possible. What an amazing feat. It proved to me that my work with Spirit was not only legitimate, but also an act of amazing realization that Spirit is capable of achieving tremendous feats and I was one of their instruments.

As I began this chapter I started by saying that the search for God is a curious adventure. I believe this statement to be true. Sometimes it takes our own experiences, mishaps and questions that lead us to some understanding of what it means to be spiritual. For me, I found my spirituality defined through my experiences with Spirit. The truth is, it doesn't take a medium to tell anyone that their loved ones live on. This is a realization that lives in the heart of all individuals. We believe it, more so, since we hope it to be true. Mediums are, essentially, the individuals who can show you proof that your loved ones are, in fact, always around and with you. If we but slow down our busy lives and look within ourselves, we can see traces, hints and glimpses of how much more there is to our physical life. Your personal spirituality is not defined by others; it can only be defined by you. When you allow yourself to explore the possibilities, there is so much to find. Your curiosity will take you many places. You will find that not only is God staring you in the face, but also he will be holding your hand and carrying you along the way. You need only allow yourself to take that journey.

Chapter Six

Contact with the Spirit World

My friends, family, co-workers and acquaintances are aware of my interest in the spirit world. Word of mouth travels fast. After all is said and done, taxes and death are two things that we can be sure of. Sooner or later you will have to deal with the questions about death when someone you care about has passed on. Society and our culture have not dealt much with the topic of death very well. The well known nurse and author Betsy Kubler Ross did much to help people understand what someone goes through when they are dying. There is very little written about spiritual experiences that families go through once their loved one passes from the physical world to the spiritual world. Sometimes, the person dying will experience contact with the spirit world before their physical death. I am often asked questions about the spirit world; therefore, I read as many books as I can on this subject. There are many wonderful people that trusted me with their spiritual stories, and they made this book possible. I thank them for the trust that they have placed in me. I am grateful for this opportunity.

I am just an ordinary, hardworking businesswoman, wife, mother, and grandmother. I am the sign of Taurus and I am known for my stubbornness and for keeping my feet firmly on the ground. I have always been aware of my responsibilities in the real, material world. It was very strange for me to be spending so much time finding out about the spirit world, a world that I never thought much about until my nephew Bobbie's death. There are so many extremely gifted persons who are not well known, yet they are incredible in their ability to heal and bring in spirit messages. Many persons are afraid to make their gift known for fear that they will be bothered constantly from those in need of comfort and help. They also fear that they will be ridiculed by those non-believers. Many of these good mediums do their mediumship in the Spiritualist Churches only. Many of the celebrity mediums of our day have nothing over the mediums that serve in these Spiritualist Churches. It still amazes me that people are willing to pay hundreds and thousands of dollars a session to communicate with a loved one in the spirit world. These same persons could go to a Spiritualist Church and wait to receive a message from their loved one free of charge. It takes patience. They will get a message when the time is right. I know of a very wealthy person who paid $5,000 to a scam artist gypsy psychic because this psychic told her she had a curse on her. The gypsy woman told her that she needed to light candles for her in order to remove the curse that was placed on her. This woman is constantly going to one psychic after another looking for answers and happiness which, ultimately, can only be found within her own being. Be very careful who you go to and run when the psychic or medium starts talking about negativity and curses. A good psychic or medium will only tell you things that you can change or that will be helpful to your spiritual growth. I do not believe in telling someone that something terrible is going to happen to them unless they have the ability to possibly change or prevent the outcome. The psychic should be careful not to upset the person that they are giving a message to. There are many psychics that work for under $100 for a session. I feel that these gifted persons should be reimbursed for their time, but I also believe that they should not take advantage of people because it is a gift and a service to humankind.

My father, Antonio, had a unique experience before his passing. He had problems with aneurysms, which are weakened arteries. Prior surgery had been successful, but he was going to need another to repair an aneurysm on his heart. After consulting three doctors, the family decided that this operation would be too risky. Years of heavy smoking had given him emphysema and the surgery would have put him at risk for pneumonia. Without surgery my father was given one year to live. We had a great year with my dad. About a week before my father passed on, he told us that his mother, sisters and loved ones who had passed to the spirit side of life before him, were coming to him in his dreams. My father said that they were beckoning him to come with them. These dreams were a little disturbing to him because he knew that the spirit world must be coming soon. He had never dreamt of them before in this manner. My father passed a week after these dreams. My father died in his sleep from an aneurysm in the main aorta to his heart. It was comforting to us to think that his loved ones were waiting to help him with his transition to the afterlife.

My father had been deceased a few years when my sister, Tonie Anna, became pregnant with her only son, T. J. She was in her late thirties and after ten years of marriage she was surprised to find out she was pregnant. Her labor was a difficult one and the baby was finally delivered by caesarean section. She delivered a beautiful healthy baby boy. After leaving the hospital ward and getting into a private room that evening; Tonie Anna saw a light come through her door. At first she thought someone entered the room but no one was there. Tonie felt a presence cross the room and sit beside her on the bed. She felt that her father was with her. He was there to let her know that everything would be alright with her beautiful baby boy. Tonie felt a sense of peace in knowing that she need not worry and then the light slowly drifted away. Since that time, my sister feels my father's presence a lot. When she walks, she believes that he walks beside her and impresses her mind with thoughts. It is a nice feeling to know that your spirit loved ones can still surround you with their love and communicate with you.

I do not know why some spirits are able to communicate to their loved ones here on this side of life and others are not. I believe the spirit's ability to communicate has to do with the level of spiritual

One in Spirit

growth reached while living here on the earth plane and the strength of their desire to communicate. Most spirits need to seek out mediums to act as conduits through which they can communicate to their loved ones.

My girlfriend Phyllis lost her son Jordan in a private plane crash. Jordan was flying to meet his parents in California, where they were vacationing. He survived the initial crash but passed to spirit a week later. Jordan was thirty-two when he died. He was a brilliant man, an aeronautical engineer, who worked for NASA. Jordan was so filled with life and everything he did he did with passion. Jordan was an accomplished violinist and his biggest fear, while in the hospital, was that he wouldn't be able to play any more because of the bad burns to his fingers.

Phyllis was filled with questions after her son's passing. We talked at length about our religions and our belief systems. Phyllis was of Jewish faith but took a particular interest in Spiritualism when she started experiencing physical phenomena in her home. One evening, the light bulb in the laundry area was flickering on and off. She asked her husband to please change the bulb, but he never got around to it. She decided to change the bulb herself the next time it flickered. She got on a step stool to change the bulb and found that there was no bulb in the socket. Phyllis discussed this incident with me and I told her that this type of thing was pretty common according to some of the books that I had read on this type of physical phenomena. I encouraged her to be open-minded and send Jordan encouragement with his ability to be able to communicate with her through this physical phenomenon.

Phyllis often senses Jordan's presence and she talks to him regularly. Whenever she would think about one of Jordan's friends who she had not heard from lately the phone would ring and that friend would be on the other end of the line. Phyllis attributed many coincidences and feelings she experienced with Jordan's ability to communicate with her. One day, Phyllis's daughter called to tell her that she was also experiencing physical phenomena in her apartment. Her daughter lived alone. She always left the radio on when she left the apartment because she liked coming home to music and she always left the toilet seat cover down. One particular evening when she came home, the radio was turned off and the toilet seat was up. She questioned her landlord to see if he or anyone else had been in the apartment. He said, no. Her daughter was convinced to that it had to have been her brother, Jordan.

This same day, Phyllis had been especially sad and depressed over the loss of her son. She managed to make it into the office even though she hadn't wanted to get out of bed. When she listened to her voicemail there was only static at first and then a beautiful instrumental piece of music followed by more static and then the voicemail voice telling her "end of messages." She recognized the music as that of a violin, maybe a harp and a tinkling like some kind of a bell. Phyllis is an accomplished opera singer and has many musician friends. She has played the message for them and none of them were able to identify all the instruments with any real certainty. Phyllis was sure that this was another message from her son, Jordan. Phyllis thought I might think she was crazy, but I assured her that this was not the first time I had heard a story like this. I asked her to please make a copy of the tape to help protect it from being accidentally erased. We were able to record the message to a cassette from the speaker phone at my office just a few days before the power outage, in her office, would have destroyed it forever. It was nearly a year after Jordan's passing when Phyllis heard the instrumental on a classical music station. It was the end of the theme song from the movie "Il Postino" (The Postman). Very apropos! I do not believe it was purely coincidence that this music was recorded on her machine. I feel it was left there intentionally to give some comfort to Phyllis in a very trying time. Whether it was left by an anonymous friend or her departed son we might never know, but it did give her some relief at a time when she needed it the most. I'm a firm believer that in life there are few accidents.

The National Association of Spiritual Churches has a National convention every year and I had been fortunate enough to be selected by the members of my church to represent them there. Members from all of the Spiritualist Churches meet to discuss topics important to the religion. Topics vary, and solutions are proposed and debated. There are great workshops and endless conversation with really interesting people. In 1998 when I attended I found it fascinating and truly evidential.

Mr. Roberts, then the head of the Evidence of Physical Phenomena Bureau spoke to us about a radio tape that was given to him after an automobile crash. Two young men were speeding and listening to the sound of a Credence Clearwater Revival tape. The car crashed and the two men were killed instantly. A family member needed a tape deck so he went to the junk yard to get the tape deck from the crashed vehicle. When he got home he found the Credence Clearwater Revival tape in the tape deck and played it. When he played it he heard a beautiful angelic choir interspersed with the Creedence Clearwater Revival music. The choir steps in for just seconds and then the Creedence Clearwater Revival tape continues. Slowed down, the words "too fast, too young" can be heard on the tape. The family was spooked and kept it hid in a drawer until a Spiritualist found out about it and gave it to Mr. Roberts. The tape was tested for tampering in England and Germany and none could be found. I was given a copy of this taped recording and often play it to people. Everyone who hears it can't help but be moved by it. Evidence like this is what I needed. I am generally a skeptical person who needed to be convinced again an again of spirit's ability to communicate after death. The more I would ask to be convinced the more people I would meet with evidence of what I had asked for.

I knew a woman who committed suicide while only in her twenties. This woman, I'll call her Maryanne, would watch a particular television show with the same friend every week. Not too long after Maryanne's passing that same friend was watching that show and remembering her friend when the recliner Maryanne used to sit in reclined as though someone had sat in it. After the show Maryanne's friend looked at the recliner and said, "Good night Maryanne. I'm going to bed." She described feeling Maryanne's presence with her in the room and then, the recliner that had reclined on its own went back to an upright position. Her friend felt good knowing that Maryann could still visit from the other side of life.

There are many types of spiritual phenomena. Spiritual phenomena consists of prophecy, clairvoyance, clairaudience, levitation, and automatic writing are just a few. I have had the pleasure of experiencing many of these spiritual phenomena myself. My first was with clairaudience. Clairaudience is the hearing of sounds, music, or voices not audible to normal hearing.

Several years after my father had passed away I was awakened around 2:00 A.M. and heard my dad say "Fatima, it is time to get started." What I heard was clear, short and to the point. My father spoke with a strong Portuguese accent and there was no mistaking his voice. I believe that my father was telling me that it was time to start getting the message out about life after death. This was an incredible experience, one that I look forward to having again in the future.

Clairvoyance is the perception of objects, events, or people that may not be perceived through the normal senses. Clairvoyance is also known as "clear seeing," an ability that also appears to exist within animals. On two separate occasions, very early in the morning, I awoke from a sound sleep to see ethereal figures at the foot of my bed. The first was of my grandmother. The second figure was a young boy, who I did not recognize. The forms lasted for only a few seconds, but the impression they left on me will remain forever.

Clairsentience is a super physical sense of perception. It involves the perception of smell, taste, touch, emotions, and physical sensations that contribute to an overall psychic and intuitive impression. Clairsentience is perhaps the most commonly used phenomena among psychics and mediums. This phenomena, I feel, is the most able to be developed through the practice of meditation. I often feel the presence of a spirit around me and then I am impressed with a word and from that word comes many thoughts that lead to a communication from the spirit side of life.

Intuition is a clear and direct knowing from within. We all have experienced this feeling at some time in our life. Some people call it a hunch or gut feeling. Knowing who is calling before answering the phone or deciding to take an alternate route to a familiar place only to realize there had been an accident on your regular route are both examples of our intuition at work. The more a person learns to trust their intuition the stronger it becomes.

Mediumship is communication with alleged non-physical entities, sometimes accompanied by paranormal physical phenomena. It is an ancient and universal practice. Mediumship may be developed through an incredible dedication to meditation. A person learning to develop as a medium must be consistent and focused for as long as it may take to achieve a state of consciousness capable of mediumship. I have witnessed people develop as mediums in just a few short years and others who have yet to develop after what seems a lifetime of trying. Why some people are naturally more gifted than others is a mystery. People's abilities or inabilities to tune into the vibration of the spirit world could be caused by a multitude of things. The ease with which someone may develop and the extent to which they develop, undoubtedly, has as much to do with their genetic make up as it does their devotion to meditation. People's busy lives and many stresses make it hard to find the time to quiet one's mind in an attempt to connect with our spiritual being. Learning to trust your intuition and acting on these feelings is an easier way to connect with spirit than a strict regimen of meditation. Meditation requires sitting still and quieting your mind for periods of about fifteen minutes a day. This can be difficult for many people to do. Fifteen minutes can feel like forever when you begin, but as you meditate more you find the time seems to go by more and more quickly. Often, leaving us wishing we had more of it.

    I do not consider myself a very good medium. Having said that, sometimes I amaze myself with the messages I get from Spirit. A medium can only be as good as the spirits who choose to speak through them. The medium is the instrument through which spirit communicates.

Dreams are another way in which spirit communicates with us. Often, messages can be given to us in a dream state that cannot be given to us while we are awake. The images we need to decipher the messages we get from spirit come to us in our subconscious mind, and our subconscious minds are more easily accessible while we sleep. With practice it is possible to quiet our conscious minds and allow our subconscious minds take precedence when we are asleep. This helps make it possible to better remember our dreams for decoding.

It is important to affirm that our conscious mind give way to our subconscious mind before bed. Meditation, prayer, and poetry are just a few ways to help with this. Keeping a dream journal to write down all of what you remember before you even open your eyes is also crucial in helping us make sense of our dreams. Once we are awake our conscious minds are active again pushing the images and symbols left by spirit to the back of our minds.

I have found many solutions to problems while dreaming and even gotten some pretty good ideas. The purchase of my condo on Marco Island was a direct result of my having reoccurring dreams about purchasing property in Florida. I would wake my husband night after night by talking in my sleep. When I woke I would not remember the dreams. Brian would tell me about them and what I said. I started to ask people questions about cities in Florida and was reminded of a real estate agent who had moved to Marco Island. Brian and I went to visit the island and fell in love with it. We made plans to buy a condo on island, and after the sale the dreams stopped. Purchasing that condo in 1988 has been one of the best investments we have ever made. It has served as a place where family and friends can go to relax and reenergize away from life's many stresses. It has brought us a lot of joy to have such a special place to share.

An apport is an object that materializes out of thin air or is transported through solid matter. This is a very rare and difficult phenomenon to produce. My deceased grand-mother and a little boy at the foot of the bed were as close to materialization as I have experienced.

I have a medium friend, Barbara. Barbara lost a diamond ring while vacationing in New Hampshire. She searched every inch of where she had stayed and where she had been, but she could not find the ring. Barbara feared this very special ring was lost forever. One day, seven years later, the ring just appeared on her sofa. Her youngest daughter, just seven at the time, told her that "Grammy returned this to you because you did so much for her when she was alive." From the mouths of babes sometimes come the most amazing things. Barbara told me she now feels as if the ring was given to her by her mother rather than her husband.

Barbara also shared with me this story. She had put some lotion on her hands before meeting a friend for breakfast. While eating she noticed another of her rings had gone missing. This one had been given to her by a long time companion, George, who had passed away. Once again she retraced her steps searching for the lost ring. Back at her apartment she prayed for the ring to be returned. Barbara said after that prayer she left the apartment to search some more by her car. The sun was bright and she hoped she might catch a glimpse of the sparkling ring, but she didn't find anything. Giving up she kissed the ring good-bye. At that moment she heard a voice that told her to turn around and look down. She followed the directions and where she had just been staring was the lost ring. Barbara swears she could not have missed the ring if it had been there just seconds before. These are the only two stories of apports that I have had the pleasure of hearing.

Chapter Seven

Spirits from the Other Side

Who are these spirits from the other side of life that care enough about us to step in and visit us, inspire us and guide us on our spiritual journey? It stands to reason that the first type of spirits that would care about us would be our loved ones that have passed on before us. These are spirits of people we have known in this lifetime or people whose stories of passing we are familiar with. These spirits could be grandparents, parents, husbands or wives, siblings, aunts, cousins, friends, and so on. They are stepping in to let us know that they still live and care about us. They are often able to help us. Sometimes, a spirit may come through that we hardly knew while they were here on the earth plane. The name and description of the spirit coming through may fit someone that you knew only briefly and you may be puzzled as to why they are coming to you. It may just be that this spirit has no other link to the earth plane but through you, because not everyone believes or is even open to the possibility of a spirit's ability to communicate with the living.

I will never forget an incident that involved my sister, Lucinda. She had received a message from a medium at one of the local Spiritualist Churches and she was given the name and the description of the spirit. The message came from a spirit that she was not very fond of. Lucinda refused the message and said "I never listened to this woman while she was alive and I am not going to listen to her while she is dead." We all got a chuckle out of her reaction. It is our decision whether to accept or reject a message being given by a medium. We must keep in mind that spirit retain the same personality that had when they were here. They are not all knowing because they have passed on. They may offer advice and guidance with the benefit of seeing things we can't, but they do not have all the answers. Ultimately, it is our life and we have "free will."

Some spirits are attracted to us because of the experiences that we are going through or the lines of work we have chosen. I have read that when a spirit assists another spirit or person on earth they grow spiritually as do we when we help another person or pray for a spirit who has passed. This growth is important to achieve a higher awareness while we are alive and to help with our spiritual progression after we have passed. The eighth Declaration of Principle, "We affirm that the doorway to reformation is never closed against any human soul here or hereafter," offers hope to everyone that we can continue to progress even after we have died a physical death.

Spirit may also assist us by impressing our minds by means of thought telepathy. You might sometimes get an idea or thought out of the blue. How many times have you experienced coincidences or luckily received opportunities that you would not have thought possible. When I decided to write this book, I just happened to meet a friend who just happened to design a logo that just happened to match perfectly the title I had just chosen. Another author and member of the Quincy Spiritualist Church, Louisa Clerici, called to offer her assistance and encouragement. She had just published "Sparks from the Fire of Time" and, come to find out, would be signing books in Naples, Florida at the same time I would be vacationing in Marco Island, just 30 minutes away. It's through these types of coincidences that spirit can influence our own abilities to get the things we need to progress on our spiritual journey. It takes practice to recognize when we are receiving help from spirit as oppose to the times when we are creating our own good fortune.

It is not necessary to have met or to have a blood relation to the spirits that are attracted to us. Many different types of spirit are attracted to us depending on our particular needs. Spirit guides, teachers, and masters help us when we are ready to develop a higher understanding of life. You will know when these spirits are at work because your interests will change. Things that seemed important to you may suddenly become less important. You may be drawn to certain books, clubs, and persons who share your new interests. These changes are always for the better and are helped along by spirits who share a common bond with the people they are trying to help. Just as we attract like minded people here on earth to associate with, like minded spirits are attracted to us for the same reasons. It is ultimately your responsibility and choice what path you choose. Your free will is always at work. I have always believed in guardian angels but I never would have imagined just how many spirit helpers are available to guide us on our journey of life.

When I was sixteen years old, I was driving my friends in my parents car and was nearly hit by a passing train. My three friends and I were singing to the sound of the blasting radio and never heard the train whistle, if it even sounded. The stop signs never flashed and the gates never came down. There was no sign of an oncoming train. We went right over the tracks with just a few seconds between us and the train. Our guardian angels were working overtime that day. I will never forget it as long as I live.

There are many teachers and mediums here on the earth plane who think it is important to know the names and description of their spirit teachers and masters. Some mediums spend a lot of time trying to get a name or a description for you. This can be very evidential in that a name or description might match a particular interest you have recently acquired. You may have recently developed a particularly strong interest in Native American life and can't get enough to read on the subject. This would all make a lot more sense if a medium was able to give you an Indian name or description of a guide that had stepped forward to help you. I don't feel that a name or description is the most important thing when being presented with a new spiritual guide. It is, after all, only the mediums perception and very difficult to prove one way or the other. What is most important is to recognize that there is a new teacher or guide coming through to you whether you receive a name and description or not. Just knowing someone new is there can often be evidence enough. You probably would have already felt a change in your energy and your interests. I once went to a development class and a student that I did not know brought me a warrior from the spirit side of life and described this spirit in detail. I recalled a dream in which this warrior came to me and shortly after, I met a man at another development class that looked like the warrior in my dream. This student was new at giving messages but she was extremely evidential. It was experiences like these that kept me wanting to know more.

These new experiences I was having with spirit often reminded me of things I had forgotten. One of those things was a story that my father had told me when I was just a child. My father's mother had a child who died at the age of sixteen. My grandmother mourned so long and hard for this child that one evening the child appeared to her and asked her to please stop mourning. She needed her mother to end her grieving so that she would be free to continue her spiritual journey in the afterlife knowing that her mother was going to be alright. After this my grandmother no longer mourned the loss of her daughter.

I did not remember my grandmother, Rosa Jesus but I have always felt her presence around me. When I was just an infant she would rock me and hold me in her shawl. After I was about two years old we had settled in the United States and I never revisited Portugal until after my grandmother had died. My grandmother was a devout Catholic of incredible faith. My father was one of fourteen children. They were poor peasants and worked very hard and were a proud family. Rosa Jesus never missed a day of church in her life. There is no doubt in my mind that my grandmother was much attuned to the vibration of spirit and it is not surprising to me that she sometimes steps forward from the spirit side of life to give me some wisdom or encouragement.

Spirit exists in the afterlife to expand a mental, moral and spiritual capacity. Spirits in the afterlife continue to progress along a path of enlightenment by helping to lift other spirits not as enlightened as themselves. They also reach out to the living through the use of mediums or even directly. Spirits enjoy the company of like minds. They are attracted to each other and to us out of a familiarity. They share their particular essence of peace, love, and joy with us in an attempt to help us on our soul's journey. The spirit world is a real and tangible place made up of congregating spirits, existing at varying stages of enlightenment. These spheres of enlightenment are filled with spirits at every stage of a soul's progression. While living we attune ourselves to these different spheres creating our own sphere of peace and harmony or of doom and discord.

The lower spheres are comprised of spirits who are filled with elements of an earthly condition. They haven't formed a more spiritual nature so they lack the ethereal atoms or forces that would allow them to progress. There are laws of attraction that keep these spirits from rising to a higher sphere until they have achieved a higher spiritual vibration.

Ignorance, hate, gossip, slander, suspicion, jealousy, worry and fear are just some of the earthly conditions that can keep us from progressing as enlightened spiritual beings. Because we are human, we cannot avoid these conditions, but we can refuse to get stuck in them. It is important to overcome them with good thoughts and deeds. The positive conditions that we should try to cultivate in our lives are things like love, faith, courage, generosity, justice, mercy, cooperation, and tolerance. These things worth working on because they will help you live a better life here on earth as well as in the afterlife.

If everyone believed in a spirit world and that they would be accountable for their thoughts and deeds even after they were deceased, the world would be a much better place to live. People who only live for today and have no belief in an afterlife can be dangerous because they don't believe they have anything to lose. You might hear these people say things like "When you are gone you're gone," "this is all there is," or, the saying I like the least, "life sucks and then you die." I feel sad for these people. They have nothing to look forward to and as they grow older and older they become more and more entrenched in a negative sphere of existence that will follow them even after they have died. Spiritualism has removed, for me, the mystery surrounding death. I know now that it's not to be feared. I have no fear of death. I look forward to dying with dignity, respectful of how important an event death is. Knowing that there will be spirits to help me in my transition to the other side gives me a real sense of security.

My brother-in-law was dying from cancer and he had just months to live. When his time was near, my daughter, Kimberlie had a dream that my nephew, Aleck, would come for him. She told me about her dream and I told her that when the time was right, she would have an opportunity to tell him this. A few days later, she was alone with him and told him about her dream. He said, "Kim, I know, he has already appeared to me." He died a few days later. Kimberlie has had several prophetic dreams. Once, while on vacation in Marco Island, she dreamed our dog, Deva, ate my son's iguana. I called my son and warned him about the dream and he said he would be careful to keep the dog away from his iguana. Kim told me the details of her dream and I told her not to dwell on it but to remind my son about her dream when she returned home. My son, Justin, had been watching the dog for us while we were vacationing. By the time my daughter arrived home, the dog had already eaten the iguana.

"Dreams are rudiments of the great state to come. We dream what is about to happen." – Bailey. Many great books of history and religion, including the Bible, show a belief in dreams. Plato, Goethe, Shakespeare, Thomas Edison, and other great names from history have placed prophetic value in dreams. In a dream, Mary and Joseph were warned of the cruel act of Herod, and fled with the Christ child into Egypt. Pilate's wife, through the influence of a dream, advised her husband to have nothing to do with the conviction of Christ. Joan of Arc predicted her death and received much information in her dreams. If you listen to your dreams, you are in good company.

Chapter Eight

Philosophically Speaking

In the beginning, it was the evidential messages that hooked me on the religion of Spiritualism, but later it became the philosophy that kept me coming. I had a desire to understand and utilize the natural principles that govern the workings of the universe. Once I accepted the scientific fact that we do not die but live in a spiritual world, I was ready to know more about natural law. I needed to know what our purpose was for being here on the earth plane and how I could use the universal laws to better my life. I wanted to know how I could use certain principles and laws to feel more fulfilled, in areas of love, relationships, careers, health, prosperity, beauty, peace, and harmony. I have seen people who have an understanding of these universal laws and use them to better their lives. I was ready for a change in what I felt was the next stage of my spiritual growth and understanding.

    I believe that we are here to create and to perfect ourselves on our soul's journey. We begin by using our imagination in order to manifest our desires. You might meditate on these desires, keeping in mind, that thoughts are alive. Once you focus on your wish in a positive manner and visualize the outcome, then you must take action to help manifest these thoughts. It is not necessary to believe in a specific religion or in metaphysics in order to use visualization and meditation techniques. It is only necessary to have the desire for a positive change and an open mind to try something new. The meditation technique that you choose is strictly individual and there is no right or wrong way to meditate. Some people relax to a meditation exercise of being lead down a peaceful forest path in which someone describes the beauty of the forest etc. while others like me, find it boring and annoying. I, personally, like a soft meditation tape of angelic music or listening to the birds chirp outside my window. I like soft candle light and a quiet, peaceful environment with people of like minds and good energy around me.

Natural law is both physical and spiritual. There is no break in natural law, it is continuous. The universe is composed of energy. In our physical world we see things being solid and separate from one another. On atomic and subatomic levels; however, all matter seems to be pure energy. We are all energy and everything around us is energy. We are all part of one great energy field vibrating at different speeds and densities, from quick and light to slow and dense. Thoughts are quick energy existing undetectable to the eye, but just as real as the desk or chair which exist at a much slower vibration. Your thoughts and feelings have their own magnetic field which attracts thoughts and feelings from others of a similar nature.

Thoughts are truly alive and we often experience this phenomenon whether we are aware of it or not. This connection of thought is taking place when you think of a person that you have not seen or heard from in years and suddenly the phone rings and that very person is on the line. Another result from the attraction of thoughts is evident when you find the answer to a question or the solution to a problem in a book that you just happened to look in or on a television or radio program that just happened to be on. I do not believe these events are only coincidence, but that they are rather a manifestation of thought. I believe that thoughts exist invisibly, broadcast into the atmosphere like radio waves. These waves are then received by like transmissions and a link is established between the transmitters creating a result like the chance meeting of a childhood friend just a day after thinking of them for the first time in years.

I had a neighbor who owned an antique book store and she was always asking me to stop in and visit her. One day in particular, I decided to visit her at her book store and I asked her if she had any old books on metaphysics. She said that she never carried any books on metaphysics or psychics. Just then, I noticed two books on a chair; one crossed the top of the other. I picked them up for a closer look only to find that one was the Reluctant Prophet and the other was on psychic phenomena. When I asked her about these books she said she did not know where they had came from and that she had never seen them before. She sold them to me for two dollars each and I enjoyed thoroughly passing them on for others to read. They were just what

I was looking for at the time. I do not believe that this experience was a matter of coincidence or serendipity. I believe in our ability to manifest results for ourselves through a network of thought. "When we search for what we truly need the whole universe conspires with us." – *Unknown*.

The Law of Attraction:

Our thoughts and our deeds are the creator of what we are attracted to and what is attracted to us. This Law affects us in our every day lives whether we are aware of it or not, so a responsible awareness can only help us with our souls progression. This is true here as well as in the afterlife. Negative thoughts and feelings only link us to negative results which create a negatively controlled sphere of existence. Breaking this cycle of negativity can be achieved by changing the way we think. Taking notice of the positive even when we are at our lowest is the only way to begin to attract the positive results we need to change the sphere of our existence.

Law of Control:

It is my belief that God wants what's best for all of us. God wants us to achieve the highest possible level of progression while we are here. The way we realize this is through our own thoughts. In order to find our path through our thoughts we must exhibit strong self control. It is important to always be your own person and never surrender control of yourself to another person or spirit. You must live your own life and make your own decisions. Living with the effects of these decisions is not always easy, and many times these effects are beyond our control. We cannot always be in control of material matters or conditions, but what we can always be in control of is how we think of these matters and conditions. Our thoughts are what guide us. They are our contact with spirit. A positive attitude about our self and our circumstances is of utmost importance to our spiritual health. When we succumb to emotion, the will of others, or even spirit we lose control. This loss of control can cause us to say and do things we regret. These regrets make us feel negatively about ourselves and these negative thoughts cloud our connections with spirit. To remain in control we need to practice seeing all sides of a situation before we react. When we learn to apply this skill in our daily lives, we can achieve balance and harmony in our life.

The law of control is not meant to be used to control others. Always remember that just as you have your opinion, you must allow others to have their opinions. You do not have to agree with someone to respect their right to have an opinion. You can agree to disagree without getting into a discussion about who is right or who is wrong. Controlling your actions and reactions is an important factor in maintaining your spiritual growth. Your spirit, with help from teachers, guides and masters from the spirit side of life, will guide you on your path, but you must nurture the connection to find true balance and happiness in your life.

Law of Vibration:

As a Spiritualist, I believe that all things, as well as people, have a specific vibration. Everything, in all the universe, animal, vegetable or mineral, exists within a particular vibration. Our thoughts and actions can raise or lower our vibration across the vibratory spectrum in which we exist. When you are feeling sadness or mistreating yourself or others, you lower your vibration and make it more difficult to properly connect with your inner spirit. By thinking good thoughts and treating yourself and others well, you can raise your vibration lifting yourself to a higher plane and easing the flow of information from spirit.

Spiritualism teaches us that our spirit teachers exist at much higher vibratory rates than ourselves. These guides send messages with messengers to guides on the plane below them, and that guide's messenger sends the message to the next plane etc. until it reaches the rate of vibration for which the message was intended. Each time the message travels from one plane to another, the rate of vibration also changes. It takes a lot of studying and developing before we can directly attract the vibration of teachers from the highest planes. We are the captains of our own ships determining the speed at which we progress. What we don't achieve here we must achieve on the spirit side of life. I believe that we all get to the same place in the end, some a little sooner than others.

Cause and Effect:

"As we sow, so shall we reap?" We have heard this saying preached many times many different ways. Whatever thoughts we have or actions we take have direct results for us even if we are not aware of them at the time. We know that if we don't eat right and exercise we can get sick or that if we go without sleep we will get tired. These effects seem elementary, but the law of cause and effect go much deeper than that. When we have negative thoughts or do things to hurt others we are hurting ourselves by lowering our vibration and stalling our progress. We cannot escape the effects of our thoughts and actions. If we understood this and acted accordingly we there would be less pain in our lives and the world would be changed for the better.

Unkind thoughts and deeds cause our vibration to change to a lower frequency which makes it difficult for our spirit teachers and guides to connect with us. We must always try to think good thoughts and keep mentally and physically fit in order to give our spirit the opportunity to flourish. Distancing yourself from situations or people that may cause you to do or feel negative things is imperative. The health and happiness of our spirit when it departs our physical bodies is determined by the effects of our thoughts and deeds. It is easier and wiser to rectify any ill effects of wrongdoing now than to wait until your soul returns to the spirit side of life. If you want to experience all the material world has to offer while preparing your place in the spirit world you must know and apply these spiritual laws. Our goal should be to reach for all that is higher and better for ourselves and others so that we will all have a better future.

The Laws of Order and Harmony:

With order, there shall be harmony. There is a very strict order to the spirit side of life. If we understand the law correctly it is not possible for spirits to get out of order. They are restricted by the law and educated by spirits of a higher plane if they attempt to act out of order. We are expected to stick to an order here on the earth plane as well. Through routine and discipline we can help maintain a well ordered mind and guard against confusion and misinterpretation. Only with order can there be a most magnificent harmony. A harmonious life is lived with clear connections between our spirits and minds allowing both beings to truly experience the wonders of the world. Our relationships and our thoughts, if negative, can put our minds out of order and create an inharmonic result. We must be vigilant against disorder in our lives if we want to enjoy the fruits of a harmonious life.

The Law of Compensation:

No good or bad deed goes unnoticed all are compensated for. How we are compensated is up to us. We are either rewarded or have to pay for all that we do here on earth as well as in spirit. When we give freely of ourselves and our resources we recognize positive returns. These returns are not always immediately evident and aren't always paid by the person we are helping or being kind to. Our rewards may be paid by someone else's kindness and generosity. We must guard against acting out of jealousy, resentment, and revenge because the compensation for these actions can be severely negative. Any debts we incur during this life are best paid while we are here rather than from the spirit side of life. It is never too late to make amends for a wrong we have committed or to ask for forgiveness. There is no hiding from the law of compensation. It is always at work.

There many Universal Laws which govern our everyday lives whether we are aware of them or not. An awareness of them is essential if we hope to get the most of our time here. I have tried to give you examples of laws that show how changing your way of thinking can change your life. You may look to other books for help in understanding the workings of these and other Laws.

The advice I would like to give to anyone reading this book would be to learn from the past, live in the now, and look to the future, an eternal one. Learning from the past does not mean only the things you have experienced firsthand. It may be enough to listen to someone's advice or to learn from someone else's mistakes. It is necessary to put the past behind you in order to be able to live in the now. Putting the past behind you can be a difficult thing to do, especially if you have experienced trauma either as a child or an adult. Nevertheless, we must resolve our self with our past.

Living in the now does not mean ignoring your responsibility for planning for your future. We need to be thinking of our future, just not so much that we are not thinking about and aware of the choices we are making in the now. Often we can be thinking three, four, or even more steps ahead of where we are in the present. This concentrates our attention on the future, no matter how near, and leaves us to make choices in the present on a kind of cruise control or auto pilot when it is these decisions that can most affect the shape our future takes. Focusing on the present concentrates our attention where we need it most, on the things we can affect directly. A living awareness of our present frees us from dwelling in our past and keeps us from obsessing about our future by giving us the control we need to manifest a state of enlightenment in our lives. My philosophical views and opinions are derived from the philosophy of Spiritualism and the use of the, National Spiritualist Association of Churches, Spiritualist Manual. A book I've tried to use as a guide in my every day life.

Chapter Nine

Class Development

Church development classes are small groups of about ten persons that come together for the purposes of developing their psychic and mediumistic abilities. These classes were something I had always been interested in since coming to the church. The teacher or person in charge is usually experienced in mediumship, healing, and psychic phenomena. The first class that I attended was conducted by the Pastor of the church, Marion, and her daughter, Phyllis. This was a non-members class which meant it was open to the public and a little larger than usual. There were about fifteen persons in this class. This class was held for the purpose of attuning to spirit for healing as well as mediumship. We also had a discussion period where we talked about different religions, history, spiritual phenomena and other topics of interest. I met some wonderful people there who, to this day, remain good friends of mine.

One of these people in particular was a Roman Catholic brother named Nathan. He was quite mediumistic and would often lecture about his many spiritual experiences as a man of the cloth or the histories of different religions. His interest in Spiritualism, as well as, his participation in class helped me with my feelings of guilt over leaving Catholicism. He told me that his experiences as a Catholic had been positive. They gave him the opportunity to learn many valuable lessons important to his own soul's growth. Being a Catholic brother helped him to accomplish many of his spiritual goals, but not all of them. He had been made aware of new truths and the pursuit of those truths had put him on his current path. I know Brother Nathan's path and my own had crossed for a reason. His presence gave me the assurance I needed to trust in the belief that what I was doing was not a sin. It eased my transition into Spiritualism by helping to free me from feelings of guilt. He helped me more than he ever knew. He has since passed to the spirit side of life and I have often felt his presence around me. I stayed in this class for a few years and will be eternally grateful for the guidance of Brother Nathan, Marion, Phyllis, as well as, all the students that assisted me in my early development.

After a while I started to feel that it was time for me to move on to another class. I wanted to learn more while continuing to develop my own mediumistic and healing abilities. I thought that a smaller class with more individualized attention would help me to accomplish this. My decision had been made. Now all I needed to do was wait for the right opportunity to present itself. Soon after leaving my first class, I joined another which was attended by my friend John. This class was led by the Reverend Jane McIntyre, a gifted medium whose talents include clairvoyance, clairaudience, clairsentience, and

One in Spirit

a trance. She is one of the few Spiritualists I know who was actually born into the religion. I was honored and privileged to be attending her class. Jane took her classes very seriously. They were mandatory and she would not tolerate absences without a real good excuse. She stressed the importance of keeping your appointment with the spirits wishing to communicate with you and your support and energy needed by the rest of the class. Jane could be quite the taskmaster, but she never failed to make you feel special and unique. Jane has a special charisma and when she speaks there is no doubt that spirit is speaking through her. Jane is particularly knowledgeable about the spirit world. It seemed as if she had been special ordered, for me, by the spirits themselves.

Her class consisted of about seven students. We met once a week at the same time and place. The class began with an opening prayer. Then we would recite the following healing prayer:

> We ask the unseen healing force to remove all obstruction from my mind and body and to restore me to perfect health. We ask this in all sincerity and honesty and I will do my part. We ask this unseen healing force to help both present and absent ones and to restore them to perfect health. I put my trust in the love and the power of God.

We then placed ourselves, loved ones, friends, animals, children and organizations of interests etc. in healing protection by reciting their names. After the healing session of the class we recited an affirmation three times. It went something like this: We are receptive to only the highest and the best influences. This affirmation is said in order to place us in the protection of white light keeping us safe from the influences of spirits with less character than those in the circle. We sat in darkness and were silent for about fifteen to twenty minutes. The purpose for this was to clear your mind of all worries and to attune yourself to the vibration of spirit. Then the circle would open for messages or philosophy. Anyone could give whatever they were receiving from spirit. With Jane's help, we were all receiving a lot of amazing information. There were a lot of developed mediums in the class and it was always a treat to receive a message from one of them. The messages always proved to be evidential and enlightening. When the teacher felt the session was over she would close the circle with a song and closing prayer. Jane liked everyone to have a turn at giving the opening and closing prayer. The prayer was always spontaneous and heartfelt. Jane ran her class in a manner that taught all the students proper platform decorum. She wanted us prepared incase we needed to serve the church in some capacity. A typical prayer might go something like this:

> Infinite Spirit, the God of our understanding, please bless all of us who are here this night and those who could not be with us this evening. I ask our spirit loved ones, guides, and teachers to touch in and allow us to feel their presence. We thank you for your thoughts of

wisdom and for your continued support in helping us to realize the truths that can set us free.
Amen.

The class would last about an hour and a half and we always stayed for refreshments to discuss what was given out in the circle or to have some philosophical discussion. I was meeting so many interesting people from all walks of life experiencing this same expanded reality together. It was not something I had been accustomed to.

One night of class in particular stands out more than any of the rest because spirit had provided me with the evidence I would need for that night the night before the class took place. I was still obsessed with reading books about the spirit side of life. I had purchased a set of books on the Ascended Masters and had begun reading one. There was a section in the book about this higher intelligence that had brought a particular flower, the lotus flower, to the earth plane. This particular flower, known for its beauty, was told to have a deeply spiritual significance. I was so taken by the description of what this flower represented that I wrote it down and tucked it in the book to be used later as a bookmark. The description of this flower somehow hit a cord with me. I later put the book in the car in case I got a chance to read it while I was waiting for a client. Normally, I would leave this book on the nightstand to be read before going to sleep.

That next day at class Jane said that she had a channeled message for everyone in the class. She went into a light trance and then started to bring a particular flower to everyone in the room. When she came to me I already knew what flower she would bring. She said, "Fatima, I have the lotus flower for you because of its spirituality." Then she explained the definition that so impressed me the night before. I thanked her for her message. The entire experience was totally amazing. When the class ended I went outside to the car where the book was and I brought it in. I showed everyone what I had written down the night before and I explained the reason I had it in the car. Jane said, "Isn't Spirit Wonderful!" I was so impressed.

Before I knew anything about the religion of Spiritualism I was attracted to an advertisement in the local community college catalogue which was for a one day seminar on psychic ability and channeling. I was very interested in any classes about the psychic ability and channeling was a fairly new term to me. I was so excited about this seminar that I rescheduled my appointments for the day and I signed up. I went early, with my tape recorder, eager not to miss a thing. The teacher's name was Margaret. She was probably in her forties, attractive, very pleasant and came across as very intelligent and rational. Margaret had a master's degree in sociology. The class was very informal, more like a discussion group than a class. We sat around a table while Margaret told us a little about her childhood and how she had arrived at this point in her life. She was very psychic as a child. Margaret thought her gift was not unique and that all children had this same ability. It soon became apparent that this was not true and Margaret realized she was different. Her ability was not something that here Baptist upbringing encouraged or embraced so she, intuitively, suppressed her psychic abilities. She was able to block and ignore things that would scare her or were things she did not care to deal with. She felt this stifled her ability for a while. As Margaret grew older she began to rely on her strong sense of intuition to help her make decisions in her life. The more Margaret relied on her intuition the more she developed her psychic abilities. It wasn't long before she began experiencing some pretty incredible things related to this remarkable gift. If someone close to her was about to die, she would see a spirit knight on a horse circle around her house. This is a symbol of death and she knew that the phone would soon ring to say that a neighbor, loved one, friend or family member had just died. These sights were frightening to her so she prayed not to see things like that and eventually learned to control what she saw. As time went on, Margaret met people who could help her to better understand her gift and develop it in a way that was comfortable for her. Margaret reached a point in her development where she was able to channel guides and teachers from the spirit side of life. It was this ability that she was about to demonstrate for all of us. She went into a light trance and the following message flowed right out of her as if she were reading it from a paper:

"Lessons from the Spirit Guides"
Message: Archangel Gabriel (Also present: Jesus, Archangel Michael, Horus, Melchisidek, Zanzibar, and Astare)

"Greetings and best wishes to each of you. We are open to your hearts and thoughts and extend the quietest of prayers for your desires. We state our appreciation, respect and excitement as you explore and be with your learning process as it evolves.

There is a magnitude of positive energy, love and guidance in your world today. Those in spirit are always present and are working with you to stir the embers, when you wake and when sleeping, as you shift your awareness. We create the stage for the transformation that has begun.

Each of you chose to be here at this time; each of you is valued, known and loved. Assistance is present to accompany you in the process of shedding your old skin and moving into your butterfly form. You are beginning to spread your wings; your potential is unlimited.

You are each challenged. Your questions take energy and are essential. Rather than disdaining them or feeling uncomfortable, know that your questions and searching with wisdom are to be valued. Old, outside beliefs have no power over you. Each must seek, search, and allow your own sense of inner knowing to develop.

You have, at times, considered yourself alone. You may feel lonely and misunderstood, but you are never alone. The spirit presence is with you always.

Some of you are learning to take first steps. Some are training for long distance events; some are at a resting place or plateau. All stages have value, meaning and lessons that accompany them. We are eager for each of you to test and develop the resources and techniques that will allow you to fly, to lift above your difficulties to manifest your dreams!

You have a deep longing to reach out and connect with Spirit, to know yourselves in new ways. Know that your intention is declared and known. Choose priorities as you are ready to grow; these will be given to you as you seek. There is no limit to your potential save what you put upon yourselves with your thoughts, words and with the choices that you make.

We have a great desire to assist you in extending your boundaries... to extend what is possible, to fully explore life in all its abundance, to know and to be all you came to be, to learn and to express in this lifetime.

Our love and commitment are with you. While you are never alone, we do not intrude. Be filled with peace, with acceptance and with joy.

Shalom. - June 29, 1989

Margaret had asked me to record this message on tape so that she could send a copy to everyone in the class. I was happy to do it and excited to have a copy of the channeled message. She also asked another person in the class, who knew shorthand, to transcribe it. I can remember thinking that it was strange to have someone transcribe it while I had the tape recorder rolling. The channeled message was beautiful and I could not wait to get home and listen to it again on my tape recorder. There were also other segments of the class that I felt were interesting on the same tape.

The class had come to a close and we said our good byes. Margaret gave us her telephone number in case we were interested in going on a spiritual trip that she takes to Egypt every year, receive a personal reading, go on a meditation walk, or take part in one of her many workshops.

    Driving home, my head was spinning with thoughts of what I had just experienced. I could not wait to play back my recording. To my amazement, when I played the tape everything on it was perfect except for the channeled message. That part of the tape was blank. Margaret knew what she was doing when she had asked someone in the class to transcribe the message. This had not been the first time that a channeled portion of a message did not come through on the tape.

Chapter Ten

Just a Thought Away

I believe that thoughts are alive; they exist with a purpose in the universe. The purpose is to help us manifest, in our own lives, all the things we dare dream. Ask the universe and you will receive the assistance you need to experience the extraordinary wonders of life. My family didn't always share my faith in this theory until they started practicing it and became aware of the results, probably in an effort to prove me wrong. The following incidents are just a few examples of how we have manifested things for ourselves over the years.

For approximately fifteen years, my husband and I were invited to spend Halloween in Salem, Massachusetts. This was a Halloween tradition for us and we dressed in costume. We toured the House of Seven Gables, listened to spooky stories in the various museums, walked the streets, and partied at a friend's condo in downtown Salem. Anyone who knows Salem knows that this time of year brings thousands of people from all over the nation to party and it is impossible to find a parking space. The streets are usually closed off.

We tried to leave early every year to get there before the hoards of people. Brian would always worry that we would have to leave the car far away and walk a distance to our friend's condo. Every year I would put the thought out to spirit to help us get a parking space right in front of the condo and every year without fail there would be a space waiting for us. Sometimes, we would arrive and a person would be pulling out and let us have the space. Brian would always remark on how lucky we were. I told him that luck had nothing to do with it and that spirit was helping us. I don't know whether he bought it, at the time, but he was always pleased to be close and not have to walk a long way.

I have always been such a busy person that I've had no patience for shopping. If I had to shop for someone and did not have a lot of time, I would ask spirits help in finding me the best gift at a reasonable price. This never seemed to fail. I would walk into the first store and go right to the perfect item and many times it was on sale or, even, clearance.

I had decided, last minute, to enter a float in Gloucester's forth of July Horribles Parade. This is a parade in my home town that people enter for fun to lampoon local current events or market their businesses. I was marketing a new Real Estate venture. I imagined a Disney Castle with all my young grandchildren as princesses and a friend's son as a prince. My mother, Hilda, would be the fairy god mother waving her wand and granting wishes. There would be four generations of woman on that float. These generations would include my mom, 85, me, 58, my daughter, Kim, 34, and the grandchildren, Maya, Lelia,

One in Spirit

and Kylie, all under the age of ten. I had little time to organize this because I started so late. Finding the castle was easy and my husband Brian assembled it in a snap. I asked spirit to help me find the rest of the things I would need. The first store I went to was T.J. Max and I walked right up to the perfect dresses. There were only two and they were the exact sizes of my two granddaughters. One was a size 4 and the other a 6. They were beautiful Cinderella dresses, which matched both of their striking blue eyes. As if that wasn't good enough, the dresses were in clearance for twelve dollars each. The tiaras were also no problem. The girls were a big hit in the parade. For my oldest granddaughter, Maya and her friend, I was able to find two identical shirts the same color of the banner they carried in front of the float. They were on sale as well. With just two weeks to go before the parade, I still needed to rent a trailer for the float. I had called forty people to ask if they had a trailer I could borrow or rent with no luck. Finally, I gave it up to spirit and remembered a boy who had worked in our restaurant twenty years before. His grandfather had owned a trucking business. When I called him he said he had just the trailer for my float. The float was such a success that we entered a second parade that Fourth of July, in the neighboring town of Rockport.

On another occasion, I needed a big sister gift for my granddaughter, Kylie. Her mom was just days away from delivering a little baby brother. I had the whole day to shop. I didn't think of putting the thought out to spirit for help. I decided that the perfect gift for Kylie would be a clock for her bedroom wall. Her room is blue and white, not exactly tough colors to match. I thought that this would be an easy gift to find and started at the toy and accessory stores. After going in and out of approximately ten stores I was exhausted. I was about to give up before I remembered to ask spirit for help. I quickly said "ok spirit do your thing." Immediately I saw a T.J. Max store and, against all odds, I pulled in. I have to admit I never thought I would find something in this store but I went in anyway. I went right to the back of the store and on the wall was just one big white clock with blue trim. It was a Beatrice Potter Clock with a cute little bunny rabbit on it. It was just what I was looking for and was very reasonably priced. I could not believe that it was there. It was the only wall clock in the store and it was perfect. This was almost too much for even me to believe. Needless to say, Kylie loved her clock.

 My son, Justin, had mentioned that his daughter, Lelia, needed a new box-spring and mattress. I thought I would buy one for her as part of a special present for her upcoming birthday. I also told him to put the thought out that and someone might approach him with one. He said he would. Within a week, Justin phoned to tell me that he while doing electrical work, in a woman's home in Rockport, he was asked if he knew anyone who could use a brand new twin mattress and box-spring. The woman said a family member was supposed to come and stay with them so they had purchased them but plans changed and they weren't needed. Justin couldn't believe it. He said he would be happy to pay for them but she insisted he just take them away. The box-spring and mattress were still in the plastic they had been shipped in. I think my son was beginning to believe.

When my daughter, Kimberlie, was engaged to be married, I was looking for favors for the wedding shower and had found the perfect crystal dish to put chocolates in. I purchased one to see if my daughter would like them as much as I did. She did and we went back to buy the rest. There were only a few left, not enough for the whole shower. I asked the salesperson to check the computer to for inventory in other stores, but she said that there were none available anywhere. We were both disappointed and started to search for something else to replace them. I put the thought out to spirit, to help us find an appropriate substitute. While we were roaming the store I tripped on a large box lying on the floor. I looked down at the box and decided to take a look inside. I opened the box and there were the same dishes we had come for. It was a full case. There was the exact amount we needed for the shower. The box was nowhere close to where it should have been and the sales people had no record of a missing box in their inventory records. What are the chances of that, let alone, the chances of my tripping over them? We just looked at one another in astonishment. I said, "Thank you spirit!"

My husband, Brian, had always dreamed of owning an antique corvette. He had envisioned the type, color, and year of his dream Vet. I had found a note he had written to himself. The note said: I owe myself a 1977, yellow, hard top convertible when the children are out of college. At the time, the restaurant business was not good and interest rates were at an all time low. The economy was bad and we had two children in college at the same time.

My daughter was dating a man in college whose father restored antiques. While she was visiting him at his parent's home she was surprised to see a 1977, canary yellow, hard top convertible corvette with leather seats, in perfect condition. Kim asked about the car and was told that the owner had just built a house and was looking to sell it for just $7,000.00. Kim called me on the spot. I had checked on similar vehicles and they were all more than twice that price. We both thought that this was too big of a coincidence to ignore. I decided to buy the car for his birthday. I purchased the car after having it inspected by my husband's cousin, who happened to have a garage in the same town as the restaurant we owned. That very, day the owner of the corvette drove by the restaurant while Brian was working and he commented on what a nice car it was to one of the employees. He was so shocked when the previous owner drove into the restaurant parking lot and presented him with the keys. Brian never would have expected such a generous gift, but this deal was just too good to pass up. He became so emotional by the surprise that he had to leave work. My son, Justin, covered for him.

Our church was in need of many repairs so the church board and members decided to do some major fund raising. One of these fundraisers was a raffle. One hundred tickets would be sold for $100 each. We asked people to buy our "Golden Tickets". Three prizes would be awarded. Third place would receive $500, second place $1,500, and first place $3,000. The church would make $5,000. We sold quite a few tickets in the beginning, but it was tough trying to sell the remainder of the tickets. After nearly deciding to give everyone their money back and nearly two years, we were able to sell the remaining tickets. I was being ordained soon and I thought that it would be nice to pick the winners of the raffle at my ordination. I knew that the members of the church, the non-members, friends, and family who had purchased the tickets would be there. The day of my pastoral ordination was a particularly beautiful one. The church was nicely decorated and the grounds were meticulous. The church was packed and the refreshments were plentiful. When it came time to pick the winners of the "Golden Ticket Raffle", I decided that my three grandchildren would pick them. I started with the oldest, Maya. She picked the $500 winner which was actually three winners. Three church members had purchased the ticket together. My granddaughter Lelia chose the second winner which was a single gentleman who had purchased the ticket on his own. It was now time for Kylie, my three year old granddaughter to choose the last and biggest winner. Kylie was busy coloring and said that she did not want to pick the winner. My friends, Bob and Terri, were there with their little girl, Grace and she quickly said, "I will pick the ticket." She put her hand in the bowl and picked the winning ticket. The woman who purchased the ticket had written "give the money back to the church" on it. This was the only ticket out of the one hundred tickets that left instructions to give the winnings back to the church. I could not stop thinking about this little girl who was meant to pick this winning ticket. She was adopted, by my friends, in China before travelling all the way here to pick the church's winning ticket. It warms my heart to think about this experience. We raised more than $8,000 for the church. Everything happens for a reason.

    Another time, the church was in need of an extra stove and a new refrigerator. I was able to do a few small fundraisers and purchased a refrigerator. I thought spirit might be able to help with the stove. I thought about how there might be someone who would donate the church a stove. Not long after asking for spirits help, I got a call from a customer asking me if I knew of anyone who needed a new stove. They had purchased a house from me and the kitchen was new, but they decided they wanted stainless appliances instead of the white ones. They needed to get rid of the stove. It was nearly new and it matched the refrigerator that we had just purchased perfectly. After adding a refrigerator and stove the church decided we needed a freezer. I put the thought out again and again spirit answered with a phone call from my son. He was calling to ask if I knew of anyone who needed a chest freezer. He was replacing theirs with a second refrigerator. I told him that is just what the church needed. He had no idea we were looking for a freezer.

    Spirits ability to help us realize our goals never ceases to amaze me. When my daughter, Kimberlie, was looking for a house or land to buy I told her and her fiancé to visualize the house or land that they wanted at the price they could afford while they were in bed at night. Kim and Michael did this. They visualized a building lot close to the water for a reasonable price.

After nights of visualization, Kimberlie was working on the computer and a sale by owner advertisement flashed on the screen describing a piece of land three houses from the Annisquam River. The owner was asking the city assessed value. She called me to look at it with her and asked me if I knew where this property was located. I knew right away, from the address where the land was located. It was next door to the first house my husband and I had purchased before Kim was even born. The lot had waited for her for over twenty-six years. They purchased the lot and built a beautiful new home. The lot was a great value and even had access to the river. Kimberlie is definitely a believer.

    I truly feel that if you think back on your life's experiences you will be able to identify times when you wished or asked for something and received it from, seemingly, out of thin air. This phenomenon is not merely coincidence. It is proof of spirits willingness to help us. You just need to think the thought, or wish for something and the opportunity will arise to help you manifest that thought or grant you your wish. I do not want to diminish the power of this energy by using, what may seem as, frivolous examples to some. I just want to show haw spirit can affect our lives in very ordinary ways. I have used this thought process to help with more serious issues regarding health, careers, education, and often, peace on earth. Some responses to requests take longer than others and the answers and opportunities may not always take the most obvious forms. For instance, requests for healing may actually take the form of death, because this is the only way to relieve the suffering and free the soul.

I have often been told by parents and grandparents that they have prayed and put the thought out that their children and grand children be healthy and happy. Requests of spirit on the behalf of others can be just as successful as any you request for yourself. One grandmother told me that she had visualized the right man for her granddaughter and, sure enough, the man she had visualized did come into her grand-daughter's life and they have had a happy marriage. No matter how small or large the request, it is never too late to ask for spirits help. I believe that if you acknowledge this power and use it you will be rewarded. The more you use it the stronger your bond with spirit becomes making it easier to manifest for yourself the things you need. Practice this theory and use it often.

Chapter Eleven

Coincidence or Meant to Be?

Eleven years ago Brian and I decided to scale down and build a smaller house. The children were in their last year at college and I knew that they would not be returning home. Justin and Kimberlie agreed to share an apartment in a two family house that we owned in Salem, Massachusetts. Our present house was not very large; however, the upkeep was major with an octagon in-ground pool to care for, many beautiful walls that needed to be maintained and nearly two acres of wooded grounds that my husband pruned. We were on a very steep hill and it was difficult to plow and shovel when the snow came. We wanted to move from West Gloucester to East Gloucester, but retaining our privacy was a must. We decided to sell our home and rent while we looked for a lot to purchase.

    I started our search by looking at all the land that was available in Gloucester and nothing appealed to me. One day in the Realtor Multiple Listing Service a three lot subdivision popped up on the computer. I had been in the Real Estate business for over twenty years and I had never heard of Ledge Lane. I knew that a Ledge Road existed but I had never been to Ledge Lane. I got in the car and drove there. To my astonishment, it was a beautiful subdivision on a lane with just a few existing homes. The last lot on the street was nearly two acres of land, but mostly wetlands. We would be limited as to where and what we could build on the lot. This wasn't a problem because we were looking to downsize anyway. The location was so perfect. It was the area we wanted with the privacy that we never expected to get. The price was right too! It was almost too good to be true! When Brian came home from work I told him that I had found the house lot that would be perfect for us and we drove over to the lot to take a look. He was impressed. We both agreed that this was it.

The next day I called my attorney, Paul, to ask him what he knew about this location and if he would look at the offer to purchase contract that I was putting together before we submitted it. Paul said "You do not want to touch this lot with a ten foot pole." It had been on the market for ten years. The neighbors were fighting the subdivision and they had almost put the developer out of business because of legal fees. He thought it would cost a fortune to get this lot to the point where we could build on it. There were many issues with the conservation commission, but my heart was set on this lot and I was not about to take no for an answer. I told Paul that I would put the offer together subject to it being a buildable lot within a six month period and that we would work with the developer's attorney to get things done at the owner's expense. Paul warned me that this was not going to be easy.

My sister, Anna, told me that in the eleven years of litigation with the neighbors and the developer there were over forty contracts to purchase on this lot that had expired. Our offer was accepted and we began the long process of meeting with the neighbors, meetings with the conservation committee and speaking to the neighbor's lawyers about concerns from the general neighborhood.

All three lots in the subdivision were now under agreement and all of us potential buyers were waiting for approvals from the conservation committee and for the attorneys to agree to settle the dispute between the developer and the neighborhood. The six month deadline arrived on our contract to purchase and we had to extend it. I kept calling my attorney, Paul, who is one of the best residential attorneys in the North Shore, and he kept giving me advice that I would pass on to the developer's lawyer.

At last, the day had come when all the criteria for the conservation committee had been met and the neighbors resigned themselves to the fact that the building of these homes was inevitable. We were finally ready to close the deal and begin the building process. Brian's dream was to build a Post and Beam house. He loved the look of the pine, cathedral ceilings, and the general feeling of warmth that the house had. We went to Yorke, Maine and chose a design that we changed a little to meet our needs. Brian and I could not wait to begin building. The building of this home became a long drawn out process. It was a stick built home with a lot of natural wood details which made it challenging to wire and plumb. I thought this house would never be finished. We had been renting and storing our personal belongings for almost two years. I was at my wit's end. Brian and I moved in before the house was completely finished, but we had the occupancy permit. We would finish the final touches in our own time. We were happy to be moved in. Brian and I both agreed that we would never build another house and that we would never move again. We were convinced that the next move from this house would be to the grave yard in a box!

Several months had passed and my friend, Phyllis, had asked me if I would like to join her and friend for a reading from a psychic who lived in the Boston area. There were four of them going and two friends had backed out. I called my daughter Kim and she accompanied us to Boston. The four of us sat waiting for our turns. I was the last to go. The psychic's name was Jaime. When I walked into her home office she said "Your name is Fatima, right?" I was very impressed until she told me that she had heard someone say my name earlier and that she remembered the name from her dealings with various realtors. Jaime was also a real estate broker. She gave me a reading that was very typical and I did not think it was a particularly good reading. She asked me if I had any questions. I asked her if the house that I was now in was the house that I would be in for the rest of my life. She asked me what the street address of the house was. I told her that it was 14 Ledge Lane. She immediately said no. The number of the house that you will be in for the rest of your life will be a number that when added has to equal 8, a number like 44 or 35, for example. I understood what she meant, but wasn't at all convinced she was right. Jaime then told me that within a week, I would have to stop the car to let a blind man cross the street with a stick. I would then know that what she is saying is the truth. This was so ridiculous that I could not stop laughing about it. I told everyone in the car that she was the worst psychic I had ever been to and that Brian and I would never leave our house.

Three days had gone by and I was driving down Winter Street in Salem. I stopped the car to let a man cross before realizing he was blind. He put his cane out in front of him and crossed the street. I could not believe this. I thought that it must be more than an incredible coincidence. Here was the evidence I needed to know that what Jaime said in the reading was true. Three months later I got a call from the Gloucester Assessor's office to inform me that my house number was being changed to 17 Ledge Lane. I could not believe my ears. I yelled over the phone one plus seven equal eight! She asked me what I was talking about and I felt I owed her an explanation. I told her all about the psychic reading, the blind man, and the number of the house. She was shocked and told me that her arms were covered in goose bumps. So were mine. I called my friends and my daughter to tell them that the number of my house had changed to 17 and that we were in the house that we were going to be in for the rest of our lives! Was this just a coincidence or was this experience meant to be?

My friend Barbara Dennis was born into the Spiritualist religion. She was an only child, born and raised in England. Barbara married and then moved to the United States. I met Barbara at the Swampscott Church and we became friends. She and I had attended many psychic classes and workshops together. We were both interested in developing to be mediums. Some people develop faster than others and Barbara was developing slowly. She had become ill and her health deteriorated to the point where she was put in a nursing home in Danvers. While she was in the nursing home I had brought her a basket she had won from a church raffle. She was so excited about the contents of the basket. There was a beautiful picture of the image of an angel formed in the ocean surf off Bass Rocks in Gloucester, a candle, a spiritual book, incense, and a free psychic reading. She especially loved the picture of the surf because she had had to give up her house in Gloucester. Barbara and I loved the East Gloucester area and we often walked along the back shore and Bass Rocks.

A few years had passed and I was looking for a picture I could use for my real estate business' web site. I remembered the picture of the surf angel and thought it would be perfect. A member of my church knew the woman, Mary, who had taken this photo. I called her and she asked me if my husband and I would meet with her before she made up her mind. Brian and I scheduled an appointment to meet with her. She lived just twenty minutes from us. When we arrived at her home she was so very pleasant and told us that the picture was taken from just behind our house in East Gloucester. She was

One in Spirit

in her seventies and had been a real estate broker most of her life. What a coincidence. I too have been a real estate broker most of my life. She told us that she liked to paint and that one day she was riding around the Gloucester's back shore, also known as Bass Rocks, when she had an urge to get out of the car and take a picture. She had no idea what she had captured until after it was developed. It was quite a surprise to her when she realized that the surf had formed into the image of an angel.

Mary agreed to let me use the picture in my web site. A few days later, she called and told me that she felt that I should have the rights to this picture. She wanted to sign a document which would give me all the rights to the photo. I hesitated at first and asked her if she was sure that no one in her family would like to have the rights to the photo. She said that she had spoken to her son and that he was not interested. She knew of no one that she felt should have it other than me. She told me that several years ago her son had met me while helping his friend look for a home. I had taken him and his friend through my own home that day and he felt comfortable with me having the rights to this picture. I thanked her and told her that some day I hoped that I could put the picture to good use raising money for different charities.

A week had passed and I got a call from Barbara's friend to let me know that Barbara had passed away. She asked me if I would oversee Barbara's memorial service. I told her that I would be pleased to. We scheduled an appointment to meet, along with a few of

Barbara's other friends, to discuss the poems and songs for the service.

I had agreed to meet the girls after I was to pick up the rights to the angel picture. On the way to Mary's I stopped at the florist to buy her a dozen long stemmed roses. The thought entered my mind that she may be allergic to the flowers, but I decided to take the chance anyway. When I arrived at her home she noticed the flowers and told me that she was allergic to them. She decided to keep them in the hall outside of her apartment. I put the vase of red roses up against a photo of the surf angel that she had on the wall. I thanked her and left.

I was the second to arrive at the meeting to discuss Barbara's memorial service. Joy and I waited for the other two girls to arrive. The last girl to arrive came in carrying the photo of the surf angel. It really stunned me because when I had brought the photo to Barbara a few years prior and never imagined that I would eventually be given the rights to this photo. I could not help but think that Barbara had the last laugh and that she was a true medium, after all! I told the girls the story about picking up the rights to the photo just an hour before. I went out to the car and got the papers to show them because I did not think that they really believed me. I am extremely grateful to Mary for the rights to this photo. I decided that the photo would be the perfect cover for this book. Could this all be just coincidence or was it meant to be?

When my daughter Kimberlie was pregnant with her second child we were all so excited to learn she was having a boy. We had three granddaughters already and had thought we might not get a grandson. We knew this pregnancy was our last chance because both of our children had agreed that they were not having any more children.

One beautiful Sunday afternoon Brian and I decided it would be wonderful to take our two youngest granddaughters on a train ride to Rockport. Kylie, Lelia, my daughter Kim and I took the train to Rockport and met Brian at the station. We walked all over Rockport. We got ice-creams, candy and gifts for the children. We had a really special day hanging out and talking about how nice it would be to have a boy in the family. The next day, Kim called me with some disturbing news. She had taken some routine medical tests and the doctor had called her to tell her that she was being "flagged" for a potential genetic disease that could be fatal to the baby. The doctor suggested that she take some further tests. Kim was undecided whether she wanted to risk the chance of hurting the baby with further testing. She wanted to take a little time to think about it. After several sleepless nights, she agreed that she needed further testing in order to put her mind to rest. I prayed on my rosary every night and everyone in my church was praying for us as well. I kept talking to this unborn child and telling him how much we loved him. I kept visualizing a healthy baby boy. I asked him to give us a definite sign that he was fine. I told him that I could not have his mother worrying for the rest of the pregnancy. I went with Kim to the hospital for the extra testing. Several doctors came and went. X-rays were taken and it was the nurse who noticed first that the babies hand was making a perfect "thumbs up" sign. I could not believe how clear it was. I waited to see if the doctors would notice it too. They did. Each doctor commented on the "thumbs up." I took this as a sign that our little boy was fine. Today he is a very smart and energetic boy. Is it coincidental that I asked for a sign and got one or was it meant to be?

How many times in your life have you said "That is a coincidence" and believed it? I think that it is time for us to look further into these so called coincidences and start thinking of them as manifestations of our thoughts and wishes.

Chapter Twelve

The Family is Everything

It is very important for me to take the time to pass on to my children and grandchildren some of the family values that were handed down to Brian and me by our parents. My dad Antonio and my mother Hilda had a strong Roman Catholic religious belief system. Brian's parents Warren and Pauline raised their children in the Congregationalist Protestant religion. Pauline was raised Catholic and Warren was raised Congregationalist Protestant. Pauline's mother-in-law Ester did not care for the religion of Catholicism and Pauline gave in to Ester's wishes. It is a bit ironic that Brian chose to raise his children in Catholicism to please me and his mother raised her children Congregationalist Protestant to please Ester. What goes around comes around. The very fact that we all had religion in our lives helped to make us who we are today. It does not matter to me what religion my grandchildren are as long as they have some religious background or spirituality in their lives. Spirituality is vital in order to have balance in our lives. All religions that teach love, peace, and kindness help to make our world a better place. Both Brian's and my family had the same values and were good people that helped one another.

My father came to America for a better life and so did my mother Hilda's family. I can remember my parents sending for my aunt, uncle and cousins from Portugal. This was quite a responsibility on the part of my parents. I was just a young child. I remember them discussing the responsibility of being sponsors. They were required to provide housing, get them a job and support them until they were capable of caring for themselves. We had a multi-family home so finding the apartment was the easiest of the tasks. It was difficult at times and there were many sacrifices that had to be made. We all pitched in and it was not long before our relatives were independent. My uncle and cousins started out working in the fishing industry and a local machine shop. They lived a very modest life style which enabled them to save money. This enabled them to fulfill their dream of building their own fishing vessel. My parents were very proud to have been able to help their family. This was a perfect example of family helping family and it left a lasting impression on me. I can recall one of my dad's favorite sayings which he always said in Portuguese, "A familia é tudo!" Translated into English this means "The family is everything!"

Our parents were both from fishing families. My mother was a fish packer and my dad was a fish cutter. Brian's dad, Warren, fished for many years after working in a variety of family businesses. They raised chickens, ran a service station, built fish boxes, and acted as general contractors. Both of our parents worked hard for what they had. They both had nice homes and newer automobiles. Brian started fishing with his dad when he was only twelve years old. I started babysitting for four children when I was just fourteen years old. We both grew up with a good work ethic. Our parents gave us the best that they were capable of giving us. I believe that every generation wants more for their children than what they had. This is a good thing to want for our children as long as we remember that our children's lives are theirs to live. Their lives are not just a second chance for us to do the things we wish we had done.

Brian and I have much in common when it comes to family values. We both believe in hard work and passing that tradition on to our children. My son, Justin, was twelve years old when he worked in our family restaurant and my daughter Kim was about ten when she trained at the register with me. They both learned the restaurant business and worked with us until they graduated college. Justin was able to purchase and insure a nice used car, at sixteen, with the money that he earned in the restaurant. Kimberlie also saved her money and used it for college. We worked as a family to pay for their college leaving them with no debt after graduation. Brian and I did not want them to have loans that would hinder them from purchasing a home down the road. We were filled with gratitude that we had the means to provide a good education for our children, help them with their weddings and give them a down payment on their houses. Justin and Kim were taught the value of a dollar and how to save for what they wanted. We hope that they too will teach their children this valuable lesson.

My son-in-law Michael has been a great addition to our family and he has a great appreciation for music. Michael is a guitarist, singer and song writer. He has recorded a bluesy rock CD titled *Walk Upon the Earth*. Michael is also a great cook. His meatballs and gravy and corned beef and cabbage with Irish soda bread are just a few of the things he makes so well. My daughter-in-law Lani is a social worker and the manager of a local Head Start classroom in Rockport. She is a very sensitive and compassionate person with a real gift for helping children and their families. Lani is always willing to help those who need her. Her life's work is a constant reminder of the importance of helping those persons who are less fortunate than us.

Another value that Brian and I share in common is the love of our ancestry. We have many photos of our loved ones whom have passed on to the spirit side of life. One of my favorite pictures is of his grandmother, Ester, when she was a young woman. She is dressed in a very beautiful white Victorian dress. Ester lived to be One hundred and three years old. That is longevity! I am hoping that this gene is passed on to our children and grandchildren for sure. We still have the original frame that this photo was put in. We also have Ester and her husband Warren's marriage certificate framed on our living room wall. It's an elegant document which is decorated with angels and cupids in pastel shades. An old family Bible and my father-in-law's favorite chair are two more family treasures we prize. The chair is a beautiful example of Victorian craftsmanship. My children remember their grandfather sitting in that chair and it brings back fond memories for them. We keep these things around us to remember these wonderful people and to remind us not to forget to keep their memory alive.

My grandchildren love to sleep over at our house. They call us Nanny and Pappy. Maya is our oldest granddaughter and she is a very good student and athlete with a talent for playing the piano. We love to talk about her basketball and lacrosse games or what she might be studying at the time while we make our own sundaes with all the peanut butter cups and other toppings we can fit. Maya is old enough to amuse herself whether on the computer, listening to her i-pod, or watching one of her favorite television shows. My other two granddaughters, Leila and Kylie, are just two years apart. They are more like sisters than cousins. They love that they have our undivided attention when they stay over. We play for hours with dolls that their parents played with. They play with dress up clothes, have talent shows, and play with the basketballs, tennis balls, and hockey sticks in the driveway and garage. Lelia and Kylie love to tell stories and listen to stories before going to bed. They prefer to hear true stories about themselves, their Moms and Dads, and other family members as opposed to the standard fairy tales most children love.

Telling stories is a great way to communicate with children and to get a sense of what they are thinking and where they are coming from. Children are so pure and honest. I think it would be great if, as adults, we could remain more like children in this way. Kylie enjoys hearing stories about her and her brother, Eric's, births. Kylie reminds me that she was not allowed to stay with her mom in the hospital for Eric's birth. She remembers feeling, but then talks about how cute Eric is and how The Lady in the sky put him in her mother's belly. Kylie likes to learn and use new words. Kylie once said, "When I do not behave I have to pay the consequence." I told her that consequence was a big word and asked her if she knew what it meant. She said, "When you do not mind your mother or father you have to go to your room. That punishment is the consequence!"

Lelia's mother Lani once asked her how she got to be so beautiful. Lelia said, "God painted me that way." Children say the cutest things. Lelia loves to tell stories about her friends and what goes on in school. One day, her friend, from next door, convinced her to crawl into a lobster pot. Once inside, her friend locked the lobster pot and said, "I am never letting you out!" Lelia screamed and her mother came to her rescue. Apparently her friend's teenage brother had done the same thing to her earlier in the week. Now that Lelia is a little older she makes sure to point out that she knows better than to go into anyplace someone could lock her in. It is great that she can tell this story and laugh about it. Everyone has a story to tell and sometimes the telling of these stories can be truly healing.

Kylie told me once, when she was just four, that it was a privilege and a responsibility to sleep at someone's house. Believe me, the privilege is all Brian's and mine. We enjoy our grandchildren so much and we feel as though we have more time for them than we did with our own children. We understand how valuable time is and we make the most of the time that we have with them. One never knows when their time on earth is up and so we must make the most of each day that we are given.

We need to encourage children to tell their stories. We need to listen to our children and grandchildren because we never know what we will hear or learn through this form of communication. Today too many children and parents do not take the opportunity to talk to one another and share their stories. Computers, radio, television and other forms of entertainment take the place of good old fashion conversation. Brian and I love to sit and listen to my mother who is in her late eighties and other older people tell their stories. They have a tremendous amount of knowledge to pass on. Older people are wise with experience. They do not have to be particularly educated to be worthy of passing on knowledge. The simple fact that they have lived a long life and have learned from their experiences is reason enough to listen to them. By listening to the experiences of others we learn from their failures as well as their successes.

My dad believed in the support of family and that family should never steer you in the wrong direction. Although this may not be the case in every family, it is an ideal worth striving for. We have certainly tried to continue this philosophy in our family and we hope it is carried on from generation to generation.

Sometimes, even the most insignificant of things can be the most valuable and worth passing on to your children. My mother does not drink coffee. Hilda is a tea drinker. Mom has always told us that a good cup of tea is best enjoyed after a long steep and from a good china cup. She believes the cup enhances the flavor of the tea. Whether this is true or not, it certainly is more fun to drink from a beautiful china cup and it makes the experience much more enjoyable and special. I have carried on this tradition with my family, friends, and company. My grandchildren love to have tea parties.

My mother believes in ironing everything. She even irons creases in my husband's boxers as well as ironing all our sheets. It does not matter that these things are put in the dryer and come out virtually wrinkle free anyway. One of the best memories from my childhood is of clean sheets that were dried on a clothes line outside. I still love the feel of clean stiff white sheets off the line. I must admit this is not nearly as convenient as machine drying, but on occasion I do still treat myself to that childhood memory. Sometimes the old ways are still the best ways. I do not know many people that still get down on their hands and knees to wash their floors. I don't always do it, but when I want to really give the floors a good cleaning I find it is the only way.

One of the best ways to pass on memories and traditions is through family recipes that have been passed down from generation to generation. I am trying to learn the Old Portuguese dishes and desserts that I grew up with. My father was a very good cook and made a variety of traditional dishes. Brian makes a dish we refer to as "Grammy Heath's Christmas Pudding." It has been in the family for over a hundred years and it is still cooked in an old cast iron pot that was handed down to us. This pudding takes six hours to bake. It is a very special pudding that was only prepared once a year on Christmas. I hope that this will encourage you to pass on those favorite traditions and childhood memories.

Chapter Thirteen

Our Church Family

The Swampscott Church of Spiritualism is a beautiful building with a stone foundation and expansive stained glass windows. The steeple of the church has been nicely renovated and we've just put on as a new roof. The grounds are meticulous. We have a committee, comprised of members, who consider it a labor of love to keep up the lawn and gardens. There is a large tree in front of the church and while in full bloom makes for a magical environment surrounding the church. The tree is so fragrant that it fills the front yard with its' sweet perfume and when the blossoms fall on the pathways leading into the church, it looks like a lush pink carpet. One of the Swampscott Church of Spiritualism's best assets is its location just a short distance from the ocean and beach. The majority of our church members are converts from many other religions. Our charming little church is available for weddings and all other celebrations of life, past and present, to people of all denominations.

One in Spirit

The Swampscott Church of Spiritualism has approximately a hundred members and another hundred non-members, at any one time. Our Church is an independent Church. We are not part of the National Association of Churches or The Federation Group. We are a community of like-minded people seeking to progress in our spiritual paths. The church membership is made up of persons from all walks of life. There are doctors, teachers, real estate brokers, retail persons, entrepreneurs, musicians, and more that make up our community. Amongst the many things that we all have in common, we all have an understanding that life continues after death and that communication between the Spirit World and the Earth World is possible. We also all recognize that "God" is the Universal Source no matter what name he is given. There is only one Universal Source known by many different names. We often refer to the God power or Infinite Spirit and believe that each of us is an integral part of this God Power.

Our philosophy teaches us that the path to spiritual growth and positive living is achieved by taking personal responsibility for one's own behavior. We do not believe in atonement. We believe that everyone must acknowledge their transgressions and take responsibility for them in order to reconcile them with God. Spiritualists do not believe in the, either or, rewards of heaven and punishments of hell. We believe that the doorway to reformation is never closed to any soul, here or here-after. This means that following death, all souls progress onward into the Spirit World where teachings for spiritual advancement continue.

A typical Sunday service at the Swampscott Church of Spiritualism includes:

- Meditation
- Healing by the "laying on of hands"
- Lecture on spiritual topics
- Spirit Communication
- Instrumental and voice music

Meditations are led by many different members of the church. We love to involve as many people as possible in our services and by alternating who leads the meditations is a great way to do this. Some meditations are very simple and some are more elaborate. Meditation creates the perfect environment to relax and prepare the mind and body for the blessings of spirit. The Meditation is usually no more than five minutes.

"Laying on of hands" is the method of healing that we use in our church. During this part of the service our, commissioned and certified, healers perform this age old process of healing. A commissioned healer must take classes and pass a test. They must also have a certain amount of affidavits from persons they have healed. Our other healers have been certified by the church. They have attended workshops and classes and have collected several affidavits of their healing powers. The laying on of hands is a practice found throughout the world's religions. Christian Churches have used this practice as both a symbolic and formal method of invoking the Holy Spirit during baptisms, healing services, blessings and ordinations of priests and other church officers. The laying on of hands is well documented in Jewish beliefs and practices. Old Testament priests were ordained this way. In biblical times the laying on of hands was used as a blessing or authority. We have witnessed many healings by the laying on of hands. The healing portion of the service is about twenty minutes.

The Swampscott Church of Spiritualism offers other methods of healing as well. They are available in our church throughout the week. A very popular method offered during the week is Tong Ren. This is a therapy system derived from Tom Tam, a prominent area acupuncturist and healer. This method works two ways:

- Individual Energy Healing Treatments
- Group Healing Treatments

The Tong Ren therapy system has been successful in treating many conditions that are difficult to treat with more conventional methods such as Cancer, Multiple Sclerosis, Diabetes and Parkinson's disease. Tong Ren energy healing is a therapy designed for healing a patient's internal energy system by using the collectible unconscious to remove blockages which cause disease. There are many success stories from patients that have been healed by the Tong Ren method of healing.

Reiki is another form of spiritual healing. This practice was developed in 1922 by Mikao Usui. Mikao Usui fasted for three weeks meditating on Mount Kurama, In Japan. He claimed to have received the ability to move healing energy through his palms.

The next part of the service is the lecture. The lecture is often given by Reverends and Pastors of ours and other Spiritualist Churches. Lectures may also be given by accomplished members of our community or the greater spiritual community. They lecture on a spiritual topic that may relate to our Declaration of Principles, a life altering spiritual experience, or maybe, a book that impressed the speaker. The lectures are always positive, uplifting and informative. We try to keep the lectures to about twenty minutes.

Last but not least is the spirit communication portion of the service. This is the foundation of Spiritualism. Spiritualists believe that life continues after death and that communication is possible between the Spirit World and the Earth World. It is in this portion of the service that a medium demonstrates this ability. A medium is someone who can connect with the Spirit World and relay information from spirit to the individual receiving the message or reading. Mediumship is a three way communication process involving the medium, spirit, and the person receiving the reading. The medium will go to a person in the church that he or she feels a connection with. They always ask first if they may give them a reading or a message. Once the medium has permission they will give the message that they are getting from the spirit. Our mediums, like healers, are certified and have formal education and training while others have shown an impressive ability in their current classes and workshops becoming practicing mediums. A very few of our mediums are so naturally talented their abilities have been with them since the time they were children. The purpose of mediumship is to prove the continuity of life after death. At their best, a medium should give evidence in their description of spirit that leaves no doubt as to whom that spirit is and what that spirit's relationship was to the person receiving the message.

One of the nicest parts of our church service is the instrumental and vocal music. We are fortunate to have a lot of gifted musicians and singers in the congregation. Everyone in our church is encouraged to participate in this part of the service. You do not have to have talent. You just need to have spirit!

There is time during the service devoted to announcements of church events and business, as well as, a weekly offering. In addition to the offering the church relies on scheduled events and fundraising to cover costs of maintenance and repairs. Our most popular fundraiser is "The Spiritual Festival" which happens two to three times a year. This is an event that offers private readings with mediums, psychics, tarot and angel card readers, and aura photographers. There are vendors selling jewelry, art, and other crafts. We usually have a raffle table with items donated by members of the church and a fifty-fifty raffle for cash. The theme of this event is usually Victorian and included in the price of the reading are refreshments, including finger sandwiches, homemade sweets, tea, coffee and other beverages. The cost of this event is twenty to twenty five dollars. We have other spirit communication events as well, dances, and dinners, I hope this chapter gives you an understanding of what you might expect to experience in a Spiritualist Church. You may go onto the internet and look up the locations of different Spiritualist Churches across the United States and abroad. Our church is located at 59 Burrill Street in Swampscott, Massachusetts. All are welcome!

Chapter Fourteen

The Purpose of it All

Now that you have read about my spiritual journey I challenge you to go on your own spiritual journey. Your quest for spirituality may lead you to embrace any one of the many different religions. It is my belief that there is no right religion. There are as many lessons to be learned as there are religions to teach them. Religion should make you want to be a better person. It should inspire you to live a good life and to help others. Just attending church is not enough to ensure spiritual growth. It is important to participate in your religion at all times in an effort to move forward on your spiritual path. Living selfishly and taking advantage of other people only stunts our spirituality. The consequence of this kind of life comes inevitably, when we judge ourselves and then take responsibility for how we have lived.

    The right religion is the one that you love to practice. It will make you feel good about yourself and that you are special in the eyes of God. I always come away from church with a feeling of healing and energy that lasts me the whole week. Often, the lecture is about something that I was thinking about throughout the week, but even when it isn't it is always some kind of spiritual nourishment. I always feel that church is worthwhile. I'm able to have intelligent conversations and share stories with persons who understand me and where I am coming from.

It is nice to have a religious experience that eliminates fear, control and guilt. We all make mistakes or we would not be here. It is helpful to believe that you can embolden your soul while living responsibly here on earth as well as in the spirit side of life. I believe that we are responsible for our own happiness or unhappiness while we journey on our spiritual path. I know this is not an easy principle to accept. It is easier to believe that others are the cause of our unhappiness, but this just isn't true. There are universal laws that help us to understand this concept and manifest happiness in our lives. It is reassuring to me to know that we have control over our lives and that control depends solely on our attitude. It is very important to be positive. There will always be some circumstances that are beyond our control, but we can always control whether we react negatively or positively.

The religion of Spiritualism has allowed me to get to know myself and to love myself even though I know that I am not perfect. My religion has taught me to use the spirit world to help me through my daily life. I have been able to communicate with my loved ones through mediumship. I have felt their presence and wishes and received the evidence of this in my daily life. This evidence has eliminated any fear that I may have had about death. Meditating has taught me to listen to God and spirit. Sitting quietly allows me to attune to spirit. When I pray I talk to God. When I sit in silence; I listen to God.

My hopes for you, the reader, is that this book gets you thinking about you and your higher self. The following pages include some of my favorite mediums and suggested readings from my friends and me. Ask and you shall receive the answers to the many questions that you may have. I am sure that some of these books will resonate with you. My wish is that you find happiness and that you have peace and harmony in your life.

Love and Light,
Reverend Fatima Heath

Chapter Fifteen

Some of My Favorite Mediums And Suggested Reading

I have listed a few names of mediums and titles of books that I have enjoyed reading. You may resonate with one of them and decide to look up more information about their subjects on the internet.

One of my favorite mediums of the past is **Edgar Cayce**. He was a twentieth century psychic and was known for his diagnosis and cures on health matters. There are many books on Edgar Cayce and there is a library in memory of him in Virginia Beach, Virginia.

Arthur Ford was another interesting medium. He was famous for his ability to communicate with the spirit world through a control (spirit) named Fletcher.

Andrew Jackson Davis was a nineteenth century Spiritualist and was known as the Father of Modern Day Spiritualism. There are many books and lectures by him that were dictated in trance.

Daniel Dunglas Home was a wonderful clairvoyant and was known for levitation and psycho kinesis (moving physical objects without touching them.)

The Fox sisters, Margaret and Catherine Fox, were eighteenth century mediums at the young age of twelve and fifteen. They brought about the advent of Modern Day Spiritualism.

Ruth Montgomery was one of my most liked mediums and famous for her many books about reincarnation, magnetic healing, Atlantis, Lemur, Earth changes, and visits from spirits. She communicated with her spirit guides via automatic writing by using her typewriter.

Nettie Colburn Maynard was a trance medium known for her book "Was Abraham Lincoln A Spiritualist?" This book is by far one of the very best books that I have ever read.

The following books are some of the many that have left a lasting impression on me, strengthening my belief in a Life after Death.

The Blue Island by Estelle Stead

The following books are all by Ruth Montgomery:

Aliens Among Us
Born to Heal
Companions Along the Way
Here and Here After
Herald of the New Age
A Search for the Truth
Strangers Among Us
Thresh hold to Tomorrow
A World Beyond

Sir Arthur Conan Doyle's many books about Spiritualism and Life after Death.

Embraced by the Light, by Betty J. Eddie
The Other Side, by James A. Pike
Laws of Spirit, by Dan Millman
Way of the Peaceful Warrior, by Dan Millman

I hope that you will read a few of the above books and that they will pique your interest in spirit life and the world beyond.

Hiding Man's Divinity

The God's having stolen from man his divinity, met in council to discuss where they should hide it. One suggested that it be carried to the other side of the earth and buried; but it was pointed out that man is a great wanderer and that he might find the lost treasure on the other side of the earth. Another proposed that it be dropped into the depths of the sea; but the same fear was expressed—that man, in his insatiable curiosity, might dive deep enough to find it even there. Finally, after a space of silence, the oldest and wisest of the Gods said: "Hide it in man himself as that is the last place he will ever think to look for it." And it was agreed, all seeing its subtle and wise strategy.

Man wandered over the earth for ages, searching in all places, high and low, far and near, before he thought to look within himself for the divinity he sought. At last, slowly, dimly, he began to realize that what he thought was far off, hidden in "the pathos of distance" is nearer than the breath he breathes, even in his own heart.

J. F. Newton

CPSIA information can be obtained at www.ICGtesting.com
Printed in the USA
BVOW07*1608200714

359769BV00001B/1/P

9 781598 249934